SHARON O'CONNOR'S MENUS

PICNICS

Picnic Recipes from Summer Music Festivals

Classic Ragtime

Menus and Music Productions, Inc.
Piedmont, California

Other Books in the Menus and Music Series

The Vivande Porta Via recipes on pages 171-176 are from *The Food of
Southern Italy* by Carlo Middione, published by William Morrow,
New York, New York.

Library of Congress Cataloging-in-Publication Data
O'Connor, Sharon
Menus and Music Volume VII
Picnics
Picnic Recipes from Summer Music Festivals
Classic Ragtime Music

Includes Index
1. Cookery 2. Entertaining
1. Title
94-075888
ISBN 1-883914-00-0

Menus and Music® is published by

Menus and Music Productions, Inc.
1462 66th Street
Emeryville, CA 94608
(510) 658-9100

Book and cover design by Michael Osborne Design, Inc.
Manufactured in the United States of America
10 9 8 7 6 5 4 3 2 1

Contents

Introduction

If your love of music and delicious food is matched by an enthusiasm for beautiful surroundings, take time out to highlight the summer with some bountiful picnics and exceptional summer music festivals. Expect a world of pleasure, enrichment, relaxation, and fun!

This book brings together twenty-five talented and creative chefs who are also guardians of regional heritages. They offer a remarkable array of picnic dishes—just how remarkable I learned while testing recipes for this book. One January evening's indoor picnic included a New England appetizer, Southern entrée, Western salad, and Canadian dessert! Fortunately home cooks now enjoy an availability of foods at the market that makes this type of cooking possible.

You can recreate an entire picnic menu from this book or choose dishes from several menus to create your own sampler. Mix and match the recipes with your own favorites and round out menus with bread, cheese, fruit, and other purchased items as you like. Try to balance contrasting textures and flavors. Of course, the first requirement of picnic foods is to be delicious. Ideally, they should also be prepared ahead of time, look grand, and be easy to transport, serve, and eat.

Ragtime and picnics belong to a simpler, more leisurely time, and both evoke nostalgia. Ragtime was once an international rage, and its joyful strains set a mood that touches us all. The classic ragtime recorded here may be enjoyed during your kitchen preparations, while driving to the picnic, or at the picnic site.

I hope this volume will open doors to the enjoyable world of summer music festivals. These festivals are an important segment of the American and Canadian musical world. Although outdoor concerts will never replace indoor concerts, festivals do convey the joy of music making and break down the barriers between performers and listeners in very pleasurable ways. The twenty-five festivals in this volume are just a few of the more than a thousand music festivals that take place in North America every year. Be sure to reserve lodging and concert tickets well in advance, because the lure of music and picnics enjoyed in the open air makes these festivals very popular events. You will be entertained, stimulated, and enriched.

One of my own favorite picnic memories is of a very small wicker basket, one plate, a Swiss Army knife, and some unforgettable moments over bread, cheese, paté, fruit, and wine. As my husband and I traveled through France for a week one spring, we enjoyed a picnic every day. After each picnic we gathered lilac blossoms growing wild by the side of the road, arranged them on the dashboard of our car, and drove on breathing in their fragrance. The scent of lilacs evokes an overwhelming nostalgia to this day. Since that spring, we have enjoyed picnics in grass taller than our young children, picnics at music festivals, and traditional Fourth of July family picnics in our hometown park. After the town parade, we enjoy a picnic spread on the grass as we listen to speeches, warbles by winners of the local bird-calling contest, and a concert.

Picnics are one of the great warm-weather pleasures. When it's time to start planning a picnic of your own, I hope this volume of *Menus and Music* makes it even more fun. Enjoy!

— *Sharon O'Connor*

Checklist for a Picnic

□ Plates

□ Forks, knives, spoons

□ Sharp knife and
   cutting board

□ Glasses

□ Bowls, including serving bowls

□ Mugs or cups and saucers

□ Thermos

□ Paper towels, disposable
   washcloths

□ Salt, pepper, and sugar
   cubes or packets

□ Bottle opener, corkscrew

□ Napkins

□ Tablecloth

□ Blanket or ground cloth

□ Book of poetry

□ Portable audio equipment
   or musical instruments

□ Recreational equipment
   such as balls, bats, gloves,
   racquets, frisbee, and croquet

□ Hat, sunglasses, sunblock

□ Binoculars

□ Favorite board game such as
   checkers, chess, backgammon

□ Candles, candleholders,
   and matches

□ Insect repellent

□ First aid supplies

□ Garbage bag

Music Notes

Ragtime, and the jazz that stemmed from it, may well be America's most original artistic creations, and like all good music, ragtime is essentially timeless.

This syncopated keyboard music began in a simpler time, when entertainment meant live performance. New music was spread by itinerant pianists, minstrel shows, brass bands, vaudeville teams, barber-shop patrons singing to a shoeshine boy's raggy banjo or guitar, and by the sheet music that was on almost every piano in America. The cakewalk was on the verge of becoming an international fad, and ragtime piano was developing at the same time. Ragtime had a charm, swing, and melodic lilt that America understood without reservation, and it was an overnight national obsession.

Sedalia and St. Louis, Missouri, were the birthplaces of ragtime. These two towns had a wealth of labor openings that attracted numerous African Americans. There were jobs in hotels, restaurants, barber shops, saloons, railroads, and on the levees. These towns also supported bordellos, sporting houses, and honkytonks where a pianist could play the way he pleased, and this is where ragtime was previewed in America. Pianists drifting from town to town following fairs and races were close to the sources of folk music. According to one meaning of the name, ragtime, was patched together during this period from bits of melody and harmony that all contributed.

As a young pianist and student of composition, Scott Joplin arrived in Sedalia in 1896. His *Maple Leaf Rag* was soon published by pioneer ragtime publisher John Stark. It sold more than a hundred thousand copies during its first dozen years, as ragtime skyrocketed to popularity. There was no melancholy in ragtime, and its first decade in the public eye was aptly named the "Gay Nineties." Ragtime soon swept Europe, and the French were cakewalking in the streets to *le temps du chiffon*. This gentle music that came from a deprived minority in America thrilled millions.

Ragtime's heyday was short-lived; it faded with the beginning of World War I. However, music now had a lilt and syncopation that wasn't there before, and this

9

has lived on in jazz and swing. Ragtime is now affectionately and respectfully remembered. It has only to be heard to be loved.

Scott Joplin

1868-1917
Bethena, Country Club,
Paragon Rag, Pineapple Rag

Scott Joplin was the most influential ragtime composer of all time. Born and raised in Bowie County, Texas, he was a self-taught pianist by the age of eleven.

Piano lessons and an introduction to European classical music and composition were part of his childhood training because an elderly German pianist gave him free lessons. Joplin moved to Sedalia, Missouri, in 1896, where he attended the Smith College for Negroes, taking classes in harmony and composition. His ragtime performances at the local Maple Leaf Club and his continued serious efforts in composition resulted in the publication of *Original Rags* in

Music Notes

March 1899. His second composition, *Maple Leaf Rag*, was published in September of the same year by Sedalia music publisher John Stark. Of his more than fifty publications, *Maple Leaf Rag* exerted the most influence. It has sold more than a million copies of sheet music and was the first in a long collaboration between Joplin and Stark. Without this collaboration, little of classic ragtime would have been preserved in printed scores.

After eight years of composing and teaching in St. Louis, Joplin moved to New York in 1907, the year that Stark set up a publishing office there. Most of Joplin's remaining energy was spent working on his folk opera, *Treemonisha*. Scott Joplin, the "King of Ragtime Writers," devoted his life to giving ragtime artistic distinction and making it a classic in form and content.

Bethena, subtitled *A Concert Waltz*, is a superb composition with five themes in five different keys. This beautiful piece is a rare example of a syncopated waltz, basically a three over four polyrhythm. It is recorded here as an arrangement for violin and piano. *Country Club Rag* was published in 1909 and is a development of march tunes. *Paragon Rag* contains tunes reminiscent of the plantation era, themes Joplin later used in *Treemonisha*, and a grandly triumphal ending. *Pineapple Rag* is among the finest rags ever written. Its rhythms reflect the dance steps of the buck and wing, and the rag's concluding strain anticipates the forceful rhythms of big band jazz. Both *Country Club* and *Pineapple Rag* are recorded here as arrangements for flute, violin, cello, and piano.

Louis Chauvin
1881-1908
Heliotrope Bouquet

Louis Chauvin was probably the most gifted young pianist in the St. Louis District during the city's 1904 World's Fair. Heralded as the "King of Ragtime Players," Chauvin was a prodigious talent who could play an entire musical show from memory after hearing it only once. He moved to Chicago in 1906 and soon received his last visit from his friend Scott Joplin. The result of this visit was their collaboration on *Heliotrope Bouquet*. The first two sections of the rag are by Chauvin and the last two are by Joplin. Chauvin left only three published compositions and not a single phonograph record. He died in Chicago at the age of twenty-seven. John Stark described *Heliotrope Bouquet* as "the audible poetry of motion" and published the work in 1907. In the 1920s, the theme of the rag's second section was taken for the chorus of a jazz classic, *Heebie Jeebies*, by Boyd Atkins. *Heliotrope Bouquet* is recorded here as an arrangement for flute and piano.

David Guion

1892-1981
Texas Foxtrot

David Guion was born on a ranch in Ballinger, Texas, and grew up listening to cowboy songs and dance tunes. He began piano studies at the age of four, and in his early teens often played at the town's silent movie theater, improvising music to fit the action on the screen. The *Texas Foxtrot*, published in 1915, originated in one of those Saturday night ragtime creations.

Guion also performed the classics, and in 1911 he went to Vienna to study with the famed teacher and pianist, Leopold Godowsky. When World War I broke out, Guion returned to Texas. He moved to New York in 1930 to find publishers for his compositions, transcriptions, and arrangements. His compositions combined his European training with the American folk music he had heard as a youth, and he became known as "The Texas Cowboy Composer." Guion composed piano solos, songs, a ballet, and orchestral suites and choral works.

Scott Hayden

1882-1915
Kismet Rag

Scott Hayden was born in Sedalia, Missouri and became a protégé of Scott Joplin. An excellent ragtime pianist and composer with a gift for melodic line, all of his published compositions were collaborations with Joplin. The lyrical *Kismet Rag* was published in 1913 by John Stark.

Charles Hunter

1876-1906
Possum and Taters

Charles Hunter, a white pioneer of ragtime, was born almost totally blind. He attended the School for the Blind in Nashville, where he learned the trade of piano tuning. While working at the Jesse French Piano company, he became a self-taught pianist and had some of his rags published. Hunter was transferred to St. Louis and performed in clubs and honkytonks. He contracted tuberculosis and died before reaching the age of thirty. His published rags were quite popular throughout the country and can be found on a number of early piano rolls.

Possum and Taters, a joyous rag with beautiful and surprising harmonies, was published in 1900. It is recorded here as an arrangement for violin and piano. The score is prefaced by a setting of the scene:

> *"... just after the first severe frost in the Fall. It is then that the persimmons are full ripe and the possums are all fat. Every persimmon tree has its possum, so to speak, and possum hunts are of nightly occurrence, until the persimmons are all gone. Sweet potatoes are an invariable, and frequently the only, accompaniment to a possum feast, which is always an occasion for a general gathering and great rejoicing."*

Music Notes

Joseph Lamb

1887-1960
Champagne Rag
Bohemia Rag

Lamb grew up in an Irish Catholic neighborhood in New Jersey. A self-taught pianist, he was attracted to ragtime. Then in 1907 he had a chance encounter with Scott Joplin in John Stark's office in Manhattan. Joplin liked Lamb's compositions and got Stark to publish them. After the first published rag, which listed Joplin as the "arranger," Stark published everything Lamb sent him. Lamb synthesized vari-

ous ragtime styles to create graceful, inventive, and melodic works of his own. Ragtime's strong connections to the march and cakewalk forms are apparent in the *Champagne Rag*, published in 1910. The rag's first theme has a march-like quality, while its third section has the stately and sprightly quality of the cakewalk. It is recorded here as an arrangement for flute and piano. *Bohemia Rag*, published in 1919, includes an unusual beginning starting in the

14

minor mode and ending in the major. It is recorded here as an arrangement for flute, violin, cello, and piano.

Charles Luckeyeth Roberts
1887-1968
Pork and Beans

Roberts began his career at the age of five with a vaudeville troupe that toured the country. He was an unusually short man, four feet ten inches tall, but he had long arms and massive hands that could stretch a fourteenth. Roberts was a brilliant pianist and the composer of fourteen musical comedies. George Gershwin was one of his pupils. In the 1920s, Roberts found a niche as an orchestra leader playing for socialites in Palm Beach, Newport, and New York. When World War II put an end to the big parties, Roberts purchased a restaurant in Harlem, which he ran until he retired.

Pork and Beans, named after a favorite sandwich combination, was published in 1913 and stands out in the ragtime literature for its originality. The rag's principal theme has startling dissonant chords, and the trio is famous for its rhythmic simulation of a rubber band stretching and snapping.

Adaline Shepherd
1885-1950
Pickles and Peppers

Pickles and Peppers is a rousing and well-loved composition by a gifted woman from Iowa. Published in 1906, this imaginative rag-march is the first and most famous of Shepherd's three published rags, all of high quality. William Jennings Bryan used *Pickles and Peppers* as a campaign tune during his 1908 bid for the White House.

Music Notes

Aspen Music Festival

The Restaurant at The Little Nell
Aspen, Colorado

The Aspen Music Festival brings audiences more than 150 concerts and events in the magnificent Rocky Mountains of Colorado during a nine week summer season. The festival operates in conjunction with the Aspen School of Music, which has some 180 faculty-artists in residence during the summer. Chamber music, the Aspen Chamber Symphony, Aspen Festival Orchestra, and Philharmonia concerts feature performances by the school's outstanding faculty and gifted students as well as renowned guest artists. During its nine-week season, the festival also offers master classes, lectures, open rehearsals, and musical discoveries for children. Main concerts are staged in the 1,700-seat Music Tent, which allows mountain air and spacious vistas to be part of the concert experience. Smaller concerts and events are held in the restored Wheeler Opera House, a reminder of Aspen's "Silver Queen" past. Every Saturday throughout the season, visitors enjoy picnics at the Music on the Mountain concerts on Aspen Mountain.

The following picnic was created by chef George Mahaffey of The Little Nell. The Little Nell is a luxurious mountain getaway that blends the virtues of a country inn with the amenities of a grand hotel. It has received the American Automobile Association's Five Diamond Award for three consecutive years and is a member of Relais & Chateaux. The Restaurant at The Little Nell features contemporary American cuisine with influences from around the world.

Picnic at the Aspen Music Festival

*Roasted Chicken Stuffed under
the Skin with Rosemary and Garlic*

*Penne Pasta with Artichoke Hearts,
Roasted Peppers, and Calamata Olives*

*Oriental Chicken Salad with Cashews, Shiitake
Mushrooms, and Orange-Sesame Vinaigrette*

*New Potato Salad with Red Onions,
Green Beans, and Sun-Dried Tomatoes*

*Apple-Cranberry Crumble with
Roasted Pecan Streusel*

The Restaurant at The Little Nell

Roasted Chicken Stuffed under
the Skin with Rosemary and Garlic

1 whole head garlic
1 tablespoon olive oil
1½ tablespoons fresh rosemary leaves
1½ tablespoons chopped fresh sage leaves
One 4½-to-5-pound free-range chicken
Salt and freshly ground black pepper to taste

Preheat the oven to 350°F. Cut about ½ inch off the top of the head of garlic. Place the garlic on a large sheet of aluminum foil and drizzle with ½ tablespoon of the olive oil. Seal the foil tightly around the garlic and bake in the oven for 30 to 35 minutes, or until the cloves are tender. When the garlic is cool enough to handle, squeeze the pulp out of each clove into a mixing bowl and mash together with the rosemary and sage.

Carefully insert your fingers between the skin and flesh of the chicken and gently separate and loosen the skin over the entire breast. Using your fingers, spread the garlic mixture evenly between the skin and the breast meat.

Rub the remaining ½ tablespoon of the olive oil evenly over the entire surface of the chicken. Season the chicken, inside and out, with salt and pepper. Place the chicken in a roasting pan, breast side up, and bake 1¼ hours, or until the juices run clear when a thin skewer is inserted into the thickest part of the thigh. Serve the chicken warm or cold.

Makes 4 servings

The Restaurant at The Little Nell

Penne Pasta with Artichoke Hearts, Roasted Peppers, and Calamata Olives

Juice of ½ lemon
8 medium artichokes
¼ cup olive oil
2 medium garlic cloves, minced
1 tablespoon minced shallot
1 tablespoon salt
1 teaspoon white pepper
½ cup dry white wine
1 cup chicken stock or broth
2 tablespoons lemon juice
1 tablespoon chopped fresh thyme
Grated zest of 2 lemons
3 cups penne pasta
½ cup pitted calamata olives
3 medium red bell peppers, roasted,
    peeled, seeded, and julienned
5 tablespoons extra-virgin olive oil
⅔ cup grated Parmesan cheese
2 tablespoons chopped fresh basil
Salt and freshly ground black pepper to taste

Fill a medium bowl with cold water and squeeze in the lemon juice. Snap off the leaves of each artichoke; start at the stem end and work upward in a circle until the top third or so. Cut off this portion of the leaves to reveal the fuzzy choke; scoop out the choke with a spoon and discard. Pare away the artichoke's tough outer skin with a small, sharp knife. Cut the artichoke bottoms into 8 wedges and place them in the bowl of lemon water until ready to use.

In a large skillet, heat the olive oil over high heat and sauté the drained and dried artichoke bottoms for 2 minutes. Stir in the garlic, shallot, salt, pepper, and wine, and continue sautéing until the liquid evaporates. Add the chicken stock or broth and the 2 tablespoons of lemon juice. Cook until the liquid evaporates again and the artichokes are crisp-tender. If they are not yet tender, add another ½ cup of water and cook until it evaporates. Add the thyme and lemon zest, and simmer 1 minute more. Remove from the heat and let cool.

Light a charcoal fire in an open grill or light a gas grill. Place the artichokes on a fine-mesh screen and grill for about 5 minutes, or until golden brown, turning once.

In a large pot of boiling water, cook the pasta until *al dente*; drain.

In a large bowl, toss the warm artichokes with the pasta and all the remaining ingredients until well combined. Serve warm or at room temperature.

Makes 6 to 8 servings

The Restaurant at The Little Nell

Oriental Chicken Salad with Cashews, Shiitake Mushrooms, and Orange-Sesame Vinaigrette

1 pound chicken breasts, boned and skinned

6 tablespoons chopped cashews

3 whole oranges

1 cup vegetable oil

6 cups rice noodles (available in specialty food stores)

1 cup finely sliced Napa cabbage

6 tablespoons stemmed, thinly sliced shiitake mushrooms

1½ cups arugula, red oak, baby spinach, and lolla rosa in equal parts

3 tablespoons 1-inch chive pieces

6 tablespoons Orange-Sesame Vinaigrette (recipe follows)

Light a charcoal fire in an open grill. Grill the chicken breasts for 4 minutes on each side. Let cool and slice.

Preheat the oven to 400°F. Spread the cashews on a baking sheet and bake in the oven for 10 minutes, or until golden brown; set aside.

Cut ¼ inch off the top and bottom of the oranges so they will sit upright on a cutting board. Trim away all the zest and pith and cut the oranges into segments. Set aside.

In a large sauté pan or skillet, heat the vegetable oil over high heat until there are waves in the oil. Carefully add the rice noodles, 1 cup at a time; they should expand in the oil and turn white. Using a slotted spoon, remove the noodles and drain on paper towel.

In a large bowl, combine the chicken, cashews, orange segments, noodles, and all the remaining ingredients. Toss to combine well and to coat everything with the orange sesame vinaigrette.

Makes 6 to 8 servings

Orange-Sesame Vinaigrette

2 tablespoons soy sauce
1 tablespoon rice vinegar
¼ cup orange juice
1 teaspoon chopped fresh ginger root
1 teaspoon freshly ground black pepper
1 teaspoon sugar
1½ teaspoons Tabasco sauce
1 teaspoon chopped garlic
½ cup peanut oil
1 tablespoon sesame oil

In a food processor, process the soy sauce, vinegar, orange juice, ginger, pepper, sugar, Tabasco, and garlic until well blended. With the motor running, slowly add the peanut and sesame oils in a thin stream until the mixture is emulsified.

New Potato Salad with Red Onions, Green Beans, and Sun-Dried Tomatoes

10 new potatoes, quartered
4 whole garlic cloves, peeled
4 whole shallots, peeled and cut in half
¼ cup virgin olive oil
Salt and pepper to taste
1 cup green beans, cooked
½ cup julienned red onion
¼ cup diced sun-dried tomatoes
3 tablespoons chopped fresh basil
3 tablespoons chopped fresh parsley

Preheat the oven to 475°F. In a large bowl, toss together the potatoes, garlic cloves, shallots, olive oil, salt, and pepper. Place in a roasting pan, cover with aluminum foil, and bake in the preheated oven for 45 minutes, or until the potatoes are tender when pierced with a fork. Let cool, then transfer to a large bowl.

In a medium pot of boiling salted water, cook the beans for 6 minutes, or until *al dente*. Drain, run under cold water, and drain again. Add to the potatoes, along with all the remaining ingredients. Toss to combine well.

Makes 6 to 8 servings

The Restaurant at The Little Nell

Apple-Cranberry Crumble with
Roasted Pecan Streusel

Bake this dessert an hour or two before leaving for the picnic. Wrap it well in aluminum foil and a kitchen towel, so it can be dished up still slightly warm at the end of the feast. If you like, bring along a carton or two of fresh cream to drizzle over individual servings.

1 cup orange juice
Grated zest of 1 orange
1¼ cups sugar
¾ pound fresh cranberries
2 tablespoons unsalted butter
2 tablespoons maple syrup
2 tablespoons honey
2 tablespoons Calvados
Roasted Pecan Streusel (recipe follows)
2 cups heavy (whipping) cream (optional)
4 Macintosh or other cooking apples, peeled,
    cored, and cut into ½-inch-thick slices

In a medium saucepan, heat the orange juice, zest, and 1 cup of the sugar over high heat. Bring to a boil, lower the heat to medium, and let simmer for 10 minutes, stirring frequently. Add the cranberries and simmer for 5 minutes more. Remove from the heat and let cool.

In a saucepan, melt the butter over medium heat and add the apples, syrup, honey, and the remaining sugar. Cook until the apples are soft but not mushy, about 5 minutes. Remove from the heat and stir in the Calvados.

Preheat the oven to 400°F. Butter a 2½-quart baking dish. Stir together the apple and cranberry mixtures, and pour into the prepared baking dish. Crumble the pecan streusel over the top. Bake about 20 minutes, or until the fruit is bubbly and

The Restaurant at The Little Nell

the streusel is golden. Serve hot or lukewarm, scooped into bowls. Drizzle with cream, if you like.

Makes 6 to 8 servings

Roasted Pecan Streusel

½ pound shelled pecans
12 tablespoons (1½ sticks) unsalted
   butter at room temperature
¾ cup brown sugar
2 cups unbleached all-purpose flour
1½ ounces almond paste
1 teaspoon ground cinnamon
½ teaspoon ground mace

Preheat the oven to 325°F. Spread the pecans on a baking sheet and bake in the preheated oven for 8 minutes, or until golden brown. When cool, transfer the nuts to a food processor and process until finely chopped. Carefully remove half of the nuts and set aside. Add 4 tablespoons of the butter and continue processing until a smooth paste is formed.

In a medium bowl, use your fingers to mix together the pecan paste, chopped pecans, and all the remaining ingredients until they form a crumbly mixture.

Chamber Music Northwest
Portland, Oregon

A Touch of Class Catering
Vancouver, Washington

Every June and July, Chamber Music Northwest presents some twenty-five chamber music concerts during a five-week season. Thirty of the nation's leading chamber musicians are in residence during the festival, and each week they perform five concerts at Reed College or the Catlin Gabel School. During open rehearsals, audiences can observe the musicians at work on their varied ensemble programs. The festival atmosphere is informal, and preconcert picnics on the college's vast lawn area are encouraged.

The following picnic was created by John Johnson of A Touch of Class Catering. A graduate of the Cordon Bleu chef school in Paris, Johnson provides catering for the Portland area and the Chamber Music Northwest festival every year.

A Picnic at Chamber Music Northwest

Chilled Salmon and Cucumber Soup

Barbecued Spareribs

Silk Salad

Teriyaki Pork on Skewers

German Beer Cake

A Touch of Class Catering

Chilled Salmon and Cucumber Soup

One 1¼-pound salmon fillet, cut into large chunks
1 onion, diced
3 cups fish stock or chicken broth
3 cucumbers, peeled, seeded, and diced
1½ to 2 tablespoons chopped fresh dill leaves
2½ cups plain yogurt
Salt and freshly ground pepper to taste
6 cucumber slices, seeded and cut in half for garnish, optional
1 green onion julienned for garnish, optional

In a steamer, steam the salmon about 8 minutes, or until just opaque in the center. Let cool, cover, and refrigerate.

In a medium saucepan, combine the onion, stock or broth, and cucumbers. Cook over low heat until the cucumbers are tender but not mushy, about 5 minutes. In a blender or food processor, purée the stock and vegetables with the dill and yogurt until smooth. Season with salt and pepper. Chill in the refrigerator until ready to pack for the picnic.

Pour the soup into bowls or cups and add the salmon. Garnish each serving with cucumber slices and green onion if desired.

Makes 6 servings

Barbecued Spareribs

These ribs may be prepared with barbecue sauce up to four days in advance and grilled the day of the picnic.

5 pounds lean spareribs, cut into 4 slabs
Salt, freshly ground black pepper, and paprika to taste

Marinade

2 garlic cloves, minced
½ cup sherry or Madeira
Juice of 1 lemon

Barbecue Sauce

2 tablespoons bacon fat or vegetable oil
2 onions, minced
½ cup finely diced celery
½ cup chopped cooked tomatoes
½ cup tomato paste
1 tablespoon prepared mustard
1 teaspoon crushed dried thyme
1 teaspoon crushed cumin seed
2 tablespoons Worcestershire sauce
2 tablespoons sugar
2 tablespoons chili powder
2 chili peppers, minced, or ¼ teaspoon
   Tabasco sauce
1 cup vinegar

Season the spareribs with salt, pepper, and paprika, and place in a shallow glass container.

In a small bowl, crush the garlic cloves and whisk in the sherry or Madeira and lemon juice. Pour this marinade over the ribs, cover with plastic wrap, and marinate in the refrigerator for several hours or overnight, turning the spareribs once or twice.

In a sauté pan or skillet over medium heat, heat the bacon fat or vegetable oil and sauté the onions and celery until translucent, about 5 minutes. Add the tomatoes, tomato paste, mustard, thyme, cumin, Worcestershire sauce, sugar, chili powder, or Tabasco sauce, and vinegar, and stir to blend well. Raise the heat to high and boil the sauce for 2 minutes; let cool.

Rub two-thirds of the barbecue sauce over all surfaces of the ribs, reserving the remaining sauce for basting. Cover and refrigerate until ready to grill.

Light a charcoal fire in an open grill. Grill the ribs until well browned, turning and basting with the sauce every 15 minutes.

Arrange the spareribs on a plate, cool cover with plastic wrap, and store in the refrigerator. Pack the ribs in the cooler when ready to transport to the picnic site.

Makes 6 servings

Silk Salad

Salting cabbage brings out a silklike texture without cooking. Fresh ginger, mint, and pink peppercorns flavor this delicious salad.

1 large green cabbage, finely shredded
3 tablespoons coarse salt
1 red onion, sliced into rings
2 tablespoons minced fresh ginger root
½ cup fresh lemon juice
½ cup olive oil
½ cup chopped fresh mint leaves
1½ tablespoons pink peppercorns
Salt to taste

In a large bowl, sprinkle the cabbage with 2 tablespoons of the salt; let stand for 4 hours.

Meanwhile, in a small bowl sprinkle the onion with the remaining 1 tablespoon of salt, and let stand for 1 hour. Cover the cabbage and onion with ice water and let stand for 1 hour more. In a colander, rinse and drain the cabbage and onion; transfer to a large bowl and toss.

In a small bowl, whisk together the ginger, lemon juice, and olive oil. Pour the dressing over the cabbage and onion, stir in the mint, peppercorns, and salt, and toss. Chill in the refrigerator for several hours before serving.

Makes 4 servings

Teriyaki Pork on Skewers

3 pounds boneless pork, cut into 1½-inch cubes

Marinade

1 cup soy sauce
¼ cup sherry
1 garlic clove, crushed
1 teaspoon sugar

Place the pork cubes in a glass container.

In a small bowl, whisk together the marinade ingredients. Pour over the pork cubes and marinate for 3 to 4 hours in the refrigerator. Drain, reserving the marinade for basting.

Light a charcoal fire in an open grill. Arrange the meat on skewers. Grill the meat slowly until the pork is cooked through and very tender, basting frequently with the marinade.

Makes 6 servings

A Touch of Class Catering

German Beer Cake

1½ cups dark beer
1 cup molasses
½ cup butter
1½ cups raisins
3 cups sifted cake flour
1 teaspoon salt
1 teaspoon cinnamon
3 teaspoons baking powder
¼ teaspoon baking soda
¼ teaspoon nutmeg
¼ teaspoon cloves
½ cup chopped nuts

Preheat the oven to 350°F. Butter and lightly flour a 10-inch tube pan.

In a medium saucepan, combine the beer, molasses, and butter; bring to a boil, stirring until the butter is melted and the mixture is smooth. Stir in the raisins, remove from the heat, and let cool.

In a large bowl, sift together the flour, salt, cinnamon, baking powder, baking soda, nutmeg, and cloves. Gradually add the beer mixture to the dry ingredients. Fold in the nuts. Pour the batter into the prepared tube pan, and bake in the preheated oven for about 1 hour, or until a wooden tester inserted in the center comes out clean.

Makes one 10-inch cake

A Touch of Class Catering

Concord Jazz Festival
Concord, California

G. B. Ratto & Company
Oakland, California

Millions of people have enjoyed open-air summer concerts at the Concord Pavilion since it opened in 1975. Located thirty miles east of San Francisco, the giant open-air pavilion seats 3,555 people under an acre-square roof that is open on three sides. There is additional seating on the lawn for another 5,000 people.

The annual Concord Jazz Festival is a popular week-long regional event in August that has gained a national reputation. This mainstream jazz festival is the creation of Carl Jefferson, a local Concord businessman, civic leader, and avid jazz enthusiast. Symphony orchestras and the biggest names in rock and popular music fill the remainder of the Concord Pavilion's six- to seven-month summer season.

The following picnic was created by chef Jeffrey Murphy of G.B. Ratto & Company. This Italian deli stocks an amazing array of food from around the world, providing one-stop shopping for picnic ingredients. The burlap sacks, drums, and wooden bins near the entrance are reminiscent of 1890s merchandising, and the adjoining restaurant has the flavor of a Gold Rush-era hall.

Picnic at the Concord Jazz Festival

Oven Roasted Potatoes and Asparagus

Minted Tomatoes and Mostaccioli

Four-Onion Focaccia with
Prosciutto and Fresh Basil Pesto

Fresh Strawberries with
Mascarpone and Balsamic Vinegar

G. B. Ratto & Company

Oven-Roasted Potatoes and Asparagus

1 pound baby red potatoes, washed and quartered
3 heads garlic, tops trimmed
½ cup extra-virgin olive oil
¼ cup chopped fresh oregano or marjoram leaves,
   or 1 tablespoon dried oregano or marjoram
¼ cup chopped fresh thyme, or 1 tablespoon dried thyme
½ pound fresh asparagus, washed and cut into 2-inch pieces
1 red onion, thinly sliced
1 bunch green onions, chopped

Preheat the oven to 350°F. In a large bowl, mix together the potatoes, garlic heads, olive oil, and oregano or marjoram and thyme. Place in a baking pan and bake in the preheated oven for 30 minutes, or until the potatoes are tender when pierced with a knife. Drain and reserve the olive oil. Set aside the potatoes and garlic to cool.

In a medium pot of boiling salted water, boil the asparagus until crisp-tender, about 5 minutes; run under cold water, drain, and set aside. Squeeze the soft baked garlic into a small bowl and mash together with the reserved olive oil. In a large bowl, combine the potatoes, asparagus, onions, and mashed garlic and oil, and gently toss together. Serve at room temperature.

Makes 4 servings

G. B. Ratto & Company

Minted Tomatoes and Mostaccioli

1 pound pasta such as mostaccioli or penne
8 Roma tomatoes, cored and cut into sixths
½ cup extra-virgin olive oil
1 tablespoon tomato paste
¼ cup chopped fresh mint or 1 ounce dried mint
Zest and juice of 2 lemons
Crushed red pepper, salt, and freshly ground black pepper to taste

In a large pot of boiling salted water, cook the pasta until *al dente*; drain. In a large bowl, gently mix together all the ingredients.

Makes 4 to 6 servings

G. B. Ratto & Company

Four-Onion Focaccia with
Prosciutto and Fresh Basil Pesto

¾ cup plus 2 tablespoons extra-virgin olive oil
1 leek, chopped
1 red onion, diced
1 yellow onion, diced
1 bunch green onions, chopped
1¼ pounds pizza flour or other high-gluten flour
1½ tablespoons active dry yeast
Pinch of sugar
1½ cups milk, warmed to 105°F
Pesto (recipe follows)
½ pound prosciutto or other ham, very thinly sliced

In a sauté pan or skillet, heat the olive oil over medium heat and sauté the leek and the onions until translucent, about 8 minutes. Transfer to a large bowl, add the flour, and mix thoroughly.

In a small bowl, add the yeast and sugar to the warm milk; let stand until the mixture starts to bubble and foam. Add to the flour and mix together with your hands, gradually adding the remaining olive oil, until the dough is soft and smooth. When the dough is the right consistency, it will clean the sides of the bowl.

Knead the dough on a clean surface for approximately 10 minutes, or until smooth and elastic. Place the dough in an oiled bowl, cover with a towel, and let rise until it doubles in volume, about 1 hour. Punch the dough down.

Preheat the oven to 400°F. Form the dough into 2 balls; place the balls on a pizza pan or baking sheet and flatten them until they are about 10 inches in diameter. Bake in the preheated oven for 25 minutes, or until golden brown.

G. B. Ratto & Company

After the focaccia has cooled, spread the surface with pesto and top with the prosciutto or other ham. Slice into wedges or squares.

Makes 2 focaccia

Pesto

1 cup chopped fresh basil
1 clove garlic
⅓ cup extra-virgin olive oil
½ ounce pine nuts
Grated Parmesan cheese to taste

In a food processor, purée the basil, garlic, olive oil, and pine nuts. Add the grated Parmesan cheese to taste.

Makes about ½ cup

Fresh Strawberries with
Mascarpone and Balsamic Vinegar

Mascarpone is an Italian cheese similar to cream cheese.

½ pound mascarpone cheese
2 tablespoons brown sugar
1 ounce good-quality balsamic vinegar
2 baskets fresh strawberries, preferably long stemmed

In a small bowl, beat together the mascarpone, brown sugar, and vinegar; place in a sealed container for the picnic basket. At the end of the picnic, dip the strawberries in the mascarpone and enjoy!

Makes 4 to 6 servings

Des Moines Metro Opera
Indianola, Iowa

Food by LaValle
Des Moines, Iowa

The Des Moines Metro Opera was founded in 1973 and is now the leading performing arts organization in Iowa. Under the guidance of founder, director, and conductor Dr. Robert L. Larsen, the company presents three fully staged productions during a three-week summer season in June and July. Known for presenting contemporary works, the resident company is also dedicated to providing a stage for young singers trained in the United States. Festival operas are performed in English and held in the Blank Performing Arts Center in the small farming community of Indianola, fifteen miles south of Des Moines. An annual picnic for opera board members precedes one of the operas, and alfresco lunches and dinners are available before every performance in a tent adjoining the theater.

The following picnic was created by Michael R. LaValle, chef and owner of Winston's Pub & Grille, a popular restaurant in Des Moines. His company, Food by LaValle, is the exclusive caterer for the Des Moines Metro Opera.

Picnic at the Des Moines Metro Opera Summer Festival

Red Pepper and Cilantro Spread on Croustades

Smoked Pork Tenderloin on
Corn Cakes with Onion-Pepper Jelly

Chilled Corn-Pasta Ravioli with Black Bean Filling

Orange Mascarpone and Sliced Strawberries with Biscotti

44

Red Pepper and Cilantro Spread on Croustades

Simple, buttery croustades are perfect with this intensely flavored spread.

4 red bell peppers, halved or quartered, cored and seeded
2 anchovies, minced
6 oil-cured black olives, pitted
4 tablespoons balsamic vinegar
2 teaspoons butter
1 tablespoon chopped cilantro
Croustades (see page 193)

Preheat the broiler. Place the bell pepper pieces skin side up on a broiling pan and place under the broiler about 4 inches from the flame. Broil until the skins blister and turn black. Remove from the broiler and place in a paper bag. Let stand for about 30 minutes to steam. Remove the peppers from the bag and peel off the charred skins.

In a blender or food processor, purée the roasted bell peppers, anchovies, and olives with the vinegar. Transfer the mixture into a saucepan, add the butter, and bring to a boil over high heat. Reduce the heat to low and simmer for 5 to 10 minutes, stirring frequently. Remove from the heat, stir in the cilantro, and spoon the mixture into a crock or other container. Cover with plastic wrap and chill in the refrigerator until ready to pack for the picnic. To serve, spread on the croustades.

Makes about 1⅓ cups

Smoked Pork Tenderloin on
Corn Cakes with Onion-Pepper Jelly

Prepare the pork tenderloin roast the night before the picnic.

1 pound pork tenderloin
1 tablespoon olive oil
1 teaspoon minced garlic
1 teaspoon chopped rosemary
¼ teaspoon salt
¼ teaspoon freshly ground pepper
Corn Cakes (recipe follows)
Onion-Pepper Jelly (recipe follows)

Trim the tenderloin of all connective tissues. Rub the meat with the olive oil, garlic, rosemary, salt, and pepper. Smoke in a covered barbecue grill over water-soaked hardwood chips, such as hickory or mesquite, until a meat thermometer inserted in the center of the meat reaches 185°F. Do not overcook. Finish cooking by roasting in a 350°F oven, if desired. Allow to cool, then wrap the roast in plastic wrap and chill in the refrigerator overnight. Slice thinly on the diagonal.

To serve, place 2 corn cakes on each plate and arrange slices of pork loin on top. Serve with the onion-pepper jelly.

Makes 4 servings

Corn Cakes

1 cup unbleached all-purpose flour
1 cup yellow cornmeal
3 teaspoons sugar

1 teaspoon salt

2 cups milk

1 egg

1 tablespoon melted butter

½ cup dried cranberries

3 egg whites, whipped to form soft peaks

In a large bowl, combine the flour, cornmeal, sugar, and salt. Whisk in the milk, egg, and melted butter until blended. Fold in the cranberries and egg whites.

Heat a greased griddle or skillet over medium heat. Pour ¼-cup portions of the batter onto the hot griddle and cook until the surface is covered with bubbles. Flip the cakes and cook until golden brown. Cool and pack for the picnic.

To serve, place the corn cakes on plates and arrange the slices of pork loin on top. Serve with the pepper jelly.

Onion-Pepper Jelly

2 tablespoons olive oil

1 medium red onion, diced

¼ cup red wine

8 ounces pepper jelly

In a sauté pan or skillet, heat the oil over medium heat and sauté the onion until translucent, about 5 minutes. Stir in the red wine and pepper jelly. Raise the temperature to high and bring the mixture to a boil. Remove from the heat and chill in the refrigerator until ready to pack for the picnic.

Chilled Corn-Pasta Ravioli with Black Bean Filling

Black Bean Filling

½ pound black beans
½ onion, chopped
¼ cup ricotta cheese
2 tablespoons chicken broth
1 tablespoon lime juice
1 teaspoon sherry
1 garlic clove, minced
½ teaspoon cumin
½ teaspoon salt
¼ teaspoon freshly ground black pepper

Ravioli

2 ears corn
2½ cups unbleached all-purpose flour
2 eggs
Salt and pepper to taste
½ cup extra-virgin olive oil, or to taste
½ cup grated Parmesan cheese, or to taste
½ cup chopped fresh basil, or to taste
2 tomatoes, cut into small wedges

To make the filling: Rinse the beans. Place them in a large saucepan over high heat and add water to cover; bring to a boil. Boil for 2 minutes and remove from the heat. Let stand for 1 hour; drain. Add more water to cover, bring to a boil, then reduce the heat to low and simmer until tender. Drain and let cool.

In a blender or food processor, purée the beans, onion, ricotta cheese, chicken broth, lime juice, sherry, garlic, cumin, salt, and pepper in 3 batches until smooth. Combine all the batches in a large bowl and stir; set aside.

To make the ravioli: Remove the kernels from the ears of corn. In a food processor, combine the corn kernels and 2 cups of the flour; pulse the machine 12 to 15 times. Add the eggs, salt, and pepper, and process for 2 or 3 minutes, or until the kernels are finely chopped. If the mixture has a doughy consistency, slowly add more flour until a coarse, cornmeal consistency is reached. The mixture should stick together when pinched. Remove the dough from the processor bowl and form into a ball. Let rest in a bowl covered with a kitchen towel for 10 to 15 minutes.

Cut the dough into ⅓-cup pieces, and roll them out by hand or with the pasta machine. Spread the black bean mixture on half of each pasta ribbon, fold the ribbon over, and crimp the edges. Cook in boiling salted water until al dente. The ravioli will rise to the top of the water when cooked. Remove and drain. In a large bowl, gently toss the ravioli with the olive oil, Parmesan cheese, basil, and tomato wedges. Cover and chill in the refrigerator until time to pack for the picnic.

Orange Mascarpone and Sliced Strawberries with Biscotti

8 ounces mascarpone cheese
¼ cup Grand Marnier or other orange liqueur
1 teaspoon grated orange zest
Juice of 1 orange
1 cup sliced strawberries or other berries
Biscotti cookies (see page 94)

In a medium bowl, whisk together the mascarpone with the Grand Marnier, orange zest, and orange juice until fluffy. Cover and chill in the refrigerator until ready to pack for the picnic.

To assemble at the picnic site, spread the orange mascarpone onto the biscotti and top with the berries.

Makes 4 servings

The Elora Festival

The Elora Mill Inn
Elora, Ontario

The Elora Festival is a summer celebration of the musical arts focusing on choral music in both the classical and popular form. The festival programs in late July and early August also feature instrumental musicians and vocal soloists. Performers are established Canadian and international artists as well as young Canadian talent. The festival commissions new works by Canadian composers and includes an educational and young-audience component. Concerts are held in such unique settings as the Elora Quarry, St. John's Church, and the Elora Mill Country Inn.

The following picnic was created by chef Brian Holden of the Elora Mill Country Inn and Restaurant. This charming country inn is a transformed grist mill that has been carefully restored and modernized. Its massive 100-foot stone walls, some 5 feet thick at the base, rise dramatically from the edge of the Grand River where it plunges into the Elora Gorge. The inn's dining room offers an international and Canadian menu that includes fresh vegetables, in season, grown at the nearby Elora Mill Farm.

Picnic along the Grand River at the Elora Festival

Cold Strawberry and Almond Soup

Pine-Smoked Duck Salad with Grilled Vegetables

Poached Salmon Rollups with
Green Peppercorn Cream Cheese

Maple Chocolate Carrot Cake

Cold Strawberry and Almond Soup

2 quarts (8 cups) strawberries
½ cup sliced almonds
¼ cup Amaretto liqueur
¾ cup strawberry or plain yogurt
¼ cup sour cream
4 cups heavy (whipping) cream
¼ cup sugar
⅛ teaspoon ground ginger
⅛ teaspoon ground cinnamon
Fresh mint sprigs for garnish

In a blender or food processor, purée the strawberries, almonds, and Amaretto; set aside.

In a large bowl, stir together the yogurt, sour cream, heavy cream, and sugar until well blended. Fold in the puréed strawberry mixture, ginger, and cinnamon. Cover and chill in the refrigerator overnight. Pack for the picnic so that it stays cold. Serve chilled, garnished with mint sprigs.

Makes 4 to 6 servings

The Elora Mill Inn

Pine-Smoked Duck Salad with Grilled Vegetables

One 3- to 4-pound duck
Duck Marinade (recipe follows)
Pine needles, enough to cover the bottom of
   a large roasting pan with a 2- or 3-inch layer
½ to ¾ cup coarse salt
2 tablespoons black peppercorns
Vegetable Marinade (recipe follows)
1 red bell pepper, cored, seeded, and cut into ½-inch slices
1 green bell pepper, cored, seeded, and cut into ½-inch slices
1 eggplant, halved lengthwise and cut into ¼-inch-thick slices
1 carrot, peeled, julienned, and cut into 2-inch lengths
1 fennel bulb, cut into 6 to 8 pieces
1 head Boston or bibb lettuce, red leaf or oak lettuce,
   arugula, or Mizuna mustard lettuce

Remove the duck meat from the bones, leaving it in large chunks. Place the meat in a shallow dish and pour the duck marinade over it. Cover with plastic wrap and marinate in the refrigerator overnight.

Preheat the oven to 350°F, or prepare a charcoal fire in a grill. Put the pine needles in a roasting pan; they should be 2 or 3 inches deep.

Sprinkle the salt and pepper over the needles. Remove the duck from the marinade, drain, and place on a rack over the needles. (Discard the marinade.) Cover the entire pan with aluminum foil, sealing tightly to keep the smoke in.

Smoke the duck over medium heat in the preheated oven or in a covered grill over medium heat. Smoking will take about 10 to 15 minutes. Do not overcook; too much smoke will dry out the meat. Open the foil and allow the meat to cool.

In the meantime, place the chopped bell peppers, eggplant, carrot, and fennel in a large bowl and pour over the vegetable marinade; toss well to coat evenly. Marinate the vegetables for 30 minutes before grilling.

If you haven't already done so, light a charcoal fire in an open grill. Remove the vegetables from the marinade and drain, reserving the marinade for later. Grill the vegetables. After grilling, return the vegetables to the marinade, toss, and let cool. Store the grilled vegetables in the marinade until ready to serve.

Once the duck has cooled, thinly slice the meat; add to the vegetables and marinade and toss. Right before serving, remove the duck and vegetables from the marinade and drain, again reserving the marinade.

To serve, tear the lettuces into bite-size pieces and toss with some of the reserved marinade. Arrange the lettuce on plates and top with the duck and vegetables. Sprinkle on a little more marinade if desired.

Makes 4 to 6 servings

Duck Marinade

¼ cup sweet sherry
½ cup canola oil
2 tablespoons freshly squeezed orange juice
Salt and freshly ground black pepper to taste

In a medium bowl, whisk together all the ingredients.

The Elora Mill Inn

Vegetable Marinade

3 tablespoons sweet sherry
½ to ¾ cup canola oil
2 or 3 fresh basil leaves
¼ cup balsamic vinegar
Salt and freshly ground black pepper to taste

In a small bowl, whisk together all the ingredients.

Poached Salmon Rollups with
Green Peppercorn Cream Cheese

2½ pounds salmon
2 cups court bouillon (see page 233)
2 pounds cream cheese at room temperature
1 tablespoon green peppercorns
½ cup mayonnaise
Dash of lemon juice
1 bunch fresh chives, chopped
Chopped fresh dill to taste
Salt and freshly ground black pepper to taste
12 soft 7-inch flour tortilla shells
1 pint alfalfa sprouts
Pickled hot peppers for garnish

Place the salmon in a large pan and carefully cover the fish with the court bouillon. Simmer the fish over low heat until just opaque in the center. Remove the fish with a slotted spatula and drain well. Let cool.

In a medium bowl, cream together the cream cheese, green peppercorns, and chopped chives.

Using a fork, flake the salmon into a large bowl, being careful to remove any bones and skin. Add the mayonnaise, lemon juice, dill, salt, and pepper, and mix gently until thoroughly combined.

Spread each tortilla with a generous layer of the cream cheese mixture. Repeat with a layer of the salmon mixture.

To make the rollups: Place 6 of the filled tortillas directly on top of the other 6 filled tortillas. Sprinkle the top of each stack with a layer of the alfalfa sprouts. One by one gently roll up the tortillas and press to seal. Repeat with the remaining tortillas and alfalfa sprouts.

The Elora Mill Inn

To serve, cut each roll on a bias into 1½-inch slices. Arrange in a container to transport to the picnic and chill in the refrigerator until ready to pack. Garnish with pickled hot peppers.

Make 6 servings

Maple Chocolate Currot Cake

1½ cups unbleached all-purpose flour
¾ cup cocoa powder
1½ teaspoons baking powder
1 teaspoon baking soda
¼ teaspoon ground cinnamon
¼ teaspoon ground ginger
¼ teaspoon allspice
3 eggs
½ cup granulated sugar
½ cup brown sugar
½ cup maple syrup
¾ cup vegetable oil
8 ounces milk chocolate
3 cups shredded carrots
½ cup chopped toasted walnuts
Frosting (recipe follows)

Preheat the oven to 350°F. Butter and flour a 10-inch round cake pan.

In a large bowl, sift together the flour, cocoa powder, baking powder, baking soda, cinnamon, ginger, and allspice; set aside. In another large bowl, beat together the eggs. Add the sugars and maple syrup, and beat until well-blended. Whisk in the oil. In the top of a double boiler, melt the chocolate over simmering water. Fold the melted chocolate into the egg mixture. Stir in the shredded carrots. Gradually add the flour mixture into the egg mixture, beating until thoroughly blended. Stir in the chopped nuts. Pour the batter into the prepared cake pan and bake in the preheated oven for 35 to 40 minutes, or until a toothpick inserted into the center of the cake comes out clean. Cool the cake in the pan for 10 minutes; then invert it onto a rack and unmold. Cool completely before frosting.

Makes one 10-inch cake

Frosting

8 ounces cream cheese at room temperature
2 cups powdered sugar
¼ cup maple syrup
Toasted sliced almonds for decoration

   In a large bowl, cream together the cream cheese, powdered sugar, and maple syrup. Frost the sides and top of the cooled cake and decorate with toasted almonds.

Glimmerglass Opera
Cooperstown, New York

Summerwood Bed and Breakfast
Richfield Springs, New York

Glimmerglass Opera presents four operas in the rolling hills of rural upstate New York during a six-week season in July and August. Performances are held in the Alice Busch Opera Theater, whose sliding side walls open to reveal vistas of woods and meadow. A Young Artists Program, recitals, master classes, and opera previews are also part of the festival. Picnics are enjoyed before the opera on the lawn or in the West Meadow, high above the theater and overlooking Otsego Lake and nearby farmlands.

The following picnic was created by Lona Smith. Lona and George Smith are proprietors of Summerwood, a restored Queen Anne Victorian bed and breakfast listed in the National Registry of Historic Places and popular for wedding receptions and holiday parties. Operagoers can order picnics from Summerwood through the Glimmerglass Opera Guild.

Picnic at the Glimmerglass Opera

Creamy Pimento Soup

Cheese Wafers

Roast Beef in Green Peppercorn Marinade

New Potatoes in Herb Vinaigrette

Orange Rum Cake

Summerwood Bed and Breakfast

Creamy Pimento Soup

2 cans beef consommé or broth
One 4-ounce can pimentos, drained
2 cups half-and-half
2 tablespoons grated onion
Parsley sprigs or pimento strips for garnish

About 5 hours before serving, refrigerate the cans of beef consommé or broth. In a blender or a food processor, purée the pimentos with the half-and-half, and onion. Transfer to a bowl and chill in the refrigerator.

One hour before the picnic, stir together the consommé or broth and pimento mixture. Store in a sealed container for transporting.

Serve cold in mugs, garnished with parsley sprigs or strips of pimento.

Makes 5 cups, or 6 to 8 servings

Cheese Wafers

1 cup (2 sticks) butter at room temperature
Two 5-ounce jars Old English cheese spread,
   or one 10-ounce cold-pack sharp cheddar cheese spread
2½ cups sifted unbleached all-purpose flour
1 teaspoon salt
¼ teaspoon cayenne pepper
1 cup finely chopped pecans

In a medium bowl, cream together the butter and cheese until smooth. Beat in the flour, salt, and cayenne. Fold in the pecans. Form the dough into a ball and then into a 1-inch log. Wrap in plastic wrap and chill in the refrigerator.

Preheat the oven to 400°F. Slice the dough into ¼-inch-thick slices and bake in the preheated oven for 12 minutes. The cheese wafers can be stored in sealed plastic containers and frozen.

Summerwood Bed and Breakfast

Roast Beef in Green Peppercorn Marinade

Prepare the roast beef the day before the picnic. Crusty French rolls are an excellent accompaniment.

3- to 4-pound top round of beef
3 or 4 garlic cloves, halved
1 or 2 tablespoons Dijon-style mustard
¼ cup crushed green peppercorns
½ pound mushrooms, sliced
Green Peppercorn Vinaigrette (recipe follows)
1 pound fresh green beans, trimmed and cut into 1-inch pieces
Mixed lettuce leaves such as Bibb, red, or green lettuce
2 tomatoes, thinly sliced
1 red onion, thinly sliced
Fresh minced oregano and thyme for garnish

Preheat the oven to 425°F. Using a sharp knife, puncture the beef in several places and push half a garlic clove deep into each opening. Using a pastry brush, coat the meat with the mustard. Turn the roast fat-side up and sprinkle the top with crushed green peppercorns.

Place the meat on a rack in a roasting pan and bake, uncovered, in the pre-heated oven for 20 minutes per pound, or until a meat thermometer inserted in the center of the meat registers 140°F. Remove from the oven and let cool slightly. Cover with plastic wrap and chill in the refrigerator.

About 3 to 4 hours before serving, thinly slice the roast beef with a sharp knife. In a large bowl, combine the slices with the mushrooms. Pour over the green peppercorn vinaigrette, and toss to coat the beef and mushrooms evenly. Cover with plastic wrap and refrigerate.

Bring a saucepan of water to a boil and add the green beans. Simmer until the beans are just tender, about 4 or 5 minutes. Drain, rinse under cold water, and drain again. Pat dry with paper towels and set aside.

To transport, line a large container, fitted with a tight lid, with lettuce leaves. Spoon the marinated beef and mushrooms into the center. Arrange the beans, tomatoes, and onion rings around the beef. Drizzle the vegetables with a few tablespoons of the marinade. Garnish with fresh oregano and thyme. (Ingredients may be transported separately and assembled at the picnic site.)

Makes 6 to 8 servings

Green Peppercorn Vinaigrette

4 teaspoons crushed green peppercorns
½ cup red wine vinegar
1 cup vegetable oil
3 tablespoons fresh lemon juice
4 teaspoons Dijon mustard
2 teaspoons sugar
¾ teaspoon salt
¼ teaspoon freshly ground black pepper

In a small bowl, whisk together all the ingredients to form an emulsion.

Summerwood Bed and Breakfast

New Potatoes in Herb Vinaigrette

These potatoes may be prepared a day in advance.

2 pounds small red potatoes
2 tablespoons white wine vinegar or lemon juice
½ teaspoon salt
½ teaspoon dry mustard
6 to 8 tablespoons olive oil
2 tablespoons chopped fresh chives, parsley, and other fresh herbs

In a large pot of boiling salted water, gently boil the potatoes until tender when pierced with a knife; drain and let cool. Cut the potatoes into halves or quarters.

In a large bowl, whisk together the vinegar, salt, mustard, olive oil, and herbs. Add the warm potatoes and toss to coat evenly. Sprinkle with the chopped herbs and cover with plastic wrap. Chill in the refrigerator until time to transport to the picnic.

Makes 4 to 6 servings

Orange Rum Cake

This cake is best if prepared a day or two in advance so that the flavors have a chance to meld.

1 cup (2 sticks) butter at room temperature
2 cups sugar
Grated zest of 2 oranges and 1 lemon
2 eggs
2½ cups sifted unbleached all-purpose flour
2 teaspoon baking powder
1 teaspoon baking soda
½ teaspoon salt
1 cup buttermilk
1 cup chopped walnuts
Juice of 2 oranges and 1 lemon
2 tablespoons rum

Preheat the oven to 350°F and butter a 10-inch tube pan.

In a large bowl, cream the butter with an electric mixer, until fluffy. Gradually beat in 1 cup of the sugar and the grated zest. Add the eggs, 1 at a time, beating well after each addition.

In another large bowl, sift together the flour, baking powder, soda, and salt. Add alternately with the buttermilk to the butter mixture, beating after each addition. Fold in the chopped nuts. Pour the batter into the prepared pan and bake in the preheated oven for 1 hour, or until a toothpick inserted into the center comes out clean. Let the cake cool slightly in the pan and invert onto a plate.

In a medium saucepan, combine the orange and lemon juices, rum, and the remaining 1 cup of sugar; bring to a boil, stirring until the sugar dissolves completely and thickens to the consistency of a syrup. Slowly spoon the hot syrup over the cake, allowing it to soak in. Cover the cake and let stand a day before serving.

Makes one 10-inch cake

Grand Teton Music Festival

The Range Restaurant
Teton Village, Wyoming

The Grand Teton Music Festival is the summer home for classical music in the Grand Tetons, one of America's most spectacular mountain ranges. In the course of more than forty-five concerts, the festival's instrumental and vocal recitals, chamber music, and symphonic performances explore the great and enduring music of the last three hundred years. Concerts are held in the acoustically acclaimed Walk Festival Hall from the beginning of June through the end of August. The resident 175 musicians are some of the finest musicians in America. Among them are more than fifty concertmasters and principal players from the major orchestras of the world. Music director Ling Tung is the inspiration and guiding force behind the festival.

The following picnic was created by Arthur Leech, owner and chef of The Range restaurant. Fixed-price evening meals at The Range feature Leech's acclaimed interpretations of American regional cuisine.

Picnic at the Grand Teton Music Festival

Herbed Chicken Paté with Tomato Vinaigrette

Warm Salad Sausalito

Cappuccino Brownie Torte

Herbed Chicken Pâté with Tomato Vinaigrette

Prepare the pâté a day or two in advance so that the flavors develop. Serve the pâté cold with crusty bread.

2 pounds raw chicken breasts, skinned and boned
1 pint heavy (whipping) cream
2 egg whites
3 shallots, minced
Freshly ground black pepper to taste
1 tablespoon chopped fresh basil
1 tablespoon chopped fresh rosemary
1 tablespoon chopped fresh thyme
Bacon for lining and topping the paté pans
Tomato Vinaigrette (recipe follows)

Preheat the oven to 325°F. In a food processor, purée the chicken breasts. Thoroughly fold in the heavy cream and egg whites. Stir in the shallots, pepper, and herbs.

Makes 1 terrine or 6-cup loaf pan with bacon. Fill the terrine or loaf pan to the top with the chicken paté and cover the top with bacon slices. Cover the pan with aluminum foil, pricking the foil to let steam escape. Place the pans in a shallow baking dish and fill the dish with water to halfway up the sides of the pans. Bake in the preheated oven about 1½ hours, or until the internal temperature reaches 160°F. Cool, cover, and refrigerate overnight. Slice the paté at the picnic site and spoon over some of the tomato vinaigrette.

Tomato Vinaigrette

Prepare this vinaigrette several hours in advance so that the flavors will have a chance to blend.

4 ripe tomatoes
¼ cup white wine vinegar
2 teaspoons chopped fresh basil
1 teaspoon salt
Freshly ground black pepper to taste
½ cup olive oil

In a food processor or blender, purée the tomatoes and transfer to a medium bowl. Stir together the vinegar, basil, salt, and pepper. Add the olive oil slowly in a steady stream, whisking the entire time.

Makes about 2 cups

The Range Restaurant

Warm Salad Sausalito

2 heads romaine lettuce
1 cup olive oil
⅓ cup white wine vinegar
¼ cup water
1 garlic clove, minced
Freshly ground black pepper to taste
½ cup shelled pistachio nuts
½ cup golden raisins
½ cup thinly sliced sun-dried tomatoes
1 red delicious apple, thinly sliced, for garnish

In a large bowl, tear the romaine lettuce into bite-sized pieces. In a saucepan, combine all the rest of the ingredients except the apple over high heat; heat until just boiling. Pour this hot dressing over the lettuce and toss to coat the leaves thoroughly. Arrange the salad on plates and garnish with apple slices.

Makes 6 to 8 servings

Cappuccino Brownie Torte

2 ounces unsweetened chocolate
⅓ cup shortening
½ cup olive oil
2 eggs
1 cup sugar
¾ cup unbleached all-purpose flour
½ teaspoon baking powder
½ teaspoon salt
½ cup chopped walnuts
Cappuccino Butter Cream (recipe follows)

Preheat the oven to 350°F. In the top of a double boiler, melt the chocolate and shortening over simmering water, stirring constantly; set aside. In a large bowl, beat together the eggs and sugar. Stir in the flour, baking powder, salt, and nuts, and mix well. Mix in the melted chocolate and shortening mixture. Spread the batter into a greased 8-inch springform pan and bake in the preheated oven for 30 to 35 minutes, or until a toothpick inserted in the center comes out clean. Remove from the pan and cool on a rack. Frost with the cappuccino butter cream.

Makes 1 torte

Cappuccino Butter Cream

¼ pound (1 stick) unsalted butter at room temperature
¾ cup powdered sugar
1 tablespoon unsweetened cocoa powder
⅛ teaspoon cinnamon
1 tablespoon cold espresso coffee or to taste
½ tablespoon rum

In a large bowl, cream together the butter, sugar, cocoa, and cinnamon until the volume of the ingredients increases by a third. Stir in the espresso and rum and blend thoroughly. After the liquid ingredients have been added, add more powdered sugar as needed to thicken the butter cream to spreading consistency.

The Range Restaurant

Guelph Spring Festival
Guelph, Ontario

Appetizingly Yours Catering
Moffat, Ontario

Since its inception, the Guelph Spring Festival has gained attention for presenting premieres of Canadian compositions and operas and for offering diversified programming of chamber, choral, and symphonic works. The two-and-a-half-week festival in late April also offers organ competitions, master classes, dance ensembles, art exhibits, and a film series. The festival takes place in the picturesque village of Guelph, located just an hour from Toronto. The magnificent Church of Our Lady Cathedral and other community churches are used for organ and choral concerts, while larger performances are held in various halls about town.

The following picnic was created by chef Ingrid von Cube of Appetizingly Yours Catering. She enjoys creating traditional fare, working with new ingredients and recipes, and orchestrating beautiful presentations.

Picnic at the Guelph Music Festival

Crudités with Water Chestnut Dip

Gazpacho

Irish Soda Bread

Curried Chicken Salad

Roast Beef Pinwheels

Wild Rice Salad

Fresh Fruit Flan

Appetizingly Yours Catering

Crudités with Water Chestnut Dip

1½ cups sour cream
½ cup mayonnaise
¼ cup finely chopped water chestnuts
¼ cup finely chopped crystallized ginger
¼ cup minced onion
¼ cup chopped parsley
1 tablespoon soy sauce
An assortment of fresh vegetables, such as carrots, celery, radishes, green onions,
 mushrooms, snow peas, cherry tomatoes, endive, broccoli, cauliflower, seedless
 cucumbers, asparagus, red and yellow bell peppers, and zucchini

In a medium bowl, stir together the sour cream, mayonnaise, water chestnuts, ginger, onion, parsley, and soy sauce until well blended. Cover the dip, and chill it in the refrigerator for up to 5 days before serving.

On the day of the picnic, prepare the vegetables by cutting the larger ones into bite-size pieces. (Mushrooms, snow peas, endive leaves, and cherry tomatoes are served whole.) Transport the dip in a small, covered container and assemble the vegetables decoratively in a basket covered with a very damp towel. At the picnic, serve the vegetables with the water chestnut dip.

Makes 8 servings

Gazpacho

This famous chilled soup originated in Andalusía, Spain and is wonderfully refreshing during hot weather. Gazpacho keeps well in the refrigerator for several days.

2½ pounds tomatoes, cored, seeded, and cut into quarters
1½ pounds cucumbers, peeled and seeded
1 onion, cut into quarters
1 pound bell peppers in assorted colors,
   cored, seeded, and cut into quarters
1 tablespoon minced garlic
2 celery stalks
2 teaspoons salt
½ teaspoon freshly ground black pepper
½ teaspoon cayenne pepper
1 teaspoon dried oregano
¼ cup extra-virgin olive oil
2 tablespoons balsamic vinegar
2 cups tomato juice
4 tablespoons Worcestershire sauce

In a food processor, purée the tomatoes, cucumbers, onion, bell peppers, garlic, and celery. Transfer to a large bowl and stir in all the remaining ingredients. Cover with plastic wrap and refrigerate until chilled.

Makes 8 servings

Irish Soda Bread

2 cups unbleached all-purpose flour
2 cups whole wheat flour
⅓ cup brown sugar
1 tablespoon baking powder
1 teaspoon baking soda
1¼ teaspoon salt
2 large eggs
1¾ cups buttermilk
3 tablespoons melted butter
1 tablespoon poppy seeds or sesame seeds

Preheat the oven to 375°F and grease a baking sheet.

In a large bowl, stir together the flours, sugar, baking powder, baking soda, and salt. In a medium bowl, whisk together the eggs, buttermilk, and melted butter. Using a fork, briskly stir the buttermilk mixture into the dry ingredients until the dough holds together in a rough mass. On a floured surface knead the dough for 1 minute, sprinkling lightly with additional flour to prevent sticking. Shape the dough into a ball. On the prepared baking sheet, pat the dough out into a 6-inch round. With a very sharp knife, slash a large X ¼-inch deep across the top. Sprinkle the poppy or sesame seeds over the top. Bake in the preheated oven for 45 to 55 minutes, or until golden brown and crusty. Cool completely before slicing.

Makes 1 loaf

Curried Chicken Salad

Three 5-ounce chicken breasts, boned and skinned
1 cup mayonnaise
1½ to 2 tablespoons curry powder
1 celery stalk, finely chopped
4 green onions, thinly sliced
¼ cup slivered almonds
¾ cup seedless grapes or halved
   pitted cherries when in season
Lettuce or pita pockets for serving

Place the chicken in a large saucepan and add just enough water to cover it. Remove the chicken and set aside. Add salt to the water and bring it to a boil over high heat. Add the chicken and bring back to a boil. Reduce the heat to low and cook until the chicken is just firm and cooked through; do not let it boil. Remove the chicken with a slotted spoon, let cool and chop into ½-inch cubes.

In a large bowl, combine the mayonnaise and curry powder. Add the chicken cubes, celery, onions, and almonds. Stir until well-combined. Just before serving, stir in the grapes. Serve over a bed of lettuce or in pita pockets.

Makes 4 servings

Roast Beef Pinwheels

Prepare these pinwheels a day in advance.

½ cup cream cheese
1 tablespoon horseradish
Salt and freshly ground black pepper to taste
Two 10-inch flour tortillas
⅓ pound rare roast beef, sliced thin
2 leaves lettuce, chopped
1 tomato, thinly sliced
½ red onion, sliced into thin rings

In a small bowl, beat together the cream cheese, horseradish, salt, and pepper until fluffy. Spread the cream cheese mixture generously onto the tortillas, making sure to spread it right to the edges. Place 3 or 4 slices of roast beef on top. Place a small mound of chopped lettuce in the center. Add 3 or 4 tomato slices, then place a few onion rings on top of the tomato. Starting at one edge, roll up the tortilla very tightly. Wrap individually in plastic wrap and chill in the refrigerator until picnic time.

The next day, slice the tortillas on a diagonal into about 8 slices each. Serve arranged in a pinwheel design on a bed of chopped lettuce.

Makes 4 servings

Appetizingly Yours Catering

Wild Rice Salad

This salad is best made four to six hours before serving.

½ cup wild rice
½ cup long-grain or basmati rice
2½ cups water
¼ cup lemon juice
⅓ to ⅔ cup extra-virgin olive oil
½ cup finely diced red onion
2 teaspoons minced garlic
½ teaspoon salt
1 teaspoon freshly ground black pepper
1 cup chopped mint leaves
1 cup chopped parsley
4 ripe tomatoes, cored, seeded, and cut into ½-inch cubes
1 large cucumber, peeled, seeded, and cut into ½-inch cubes

Rinse the wild rice thoroughly. In a medium saucepan over high heat, bring 1½ cups of the water to a boil; add the wild rice. Reduce the heat to medium, and simmer for 40 minutes, or until the grains are tender. Drain and rinse.

In a small saucepan, bring the remaining 1 cup of water to a boil. Add the long-grain or basmati rice, cover, and reduce the heat to low. Cook for 20 minutes, or until tender.

In a large bowl, stir together the rice, lemon juice, ⅓ cup of the olive oil, onion, garlic, salt, pepper, mint, and parsley; mix well. Stir in the tomatoes and cucumber. If the salad is too dry, add a little more olive oil. Adjust the seasonings to taste. Cover and chill in the refrigerator until picnic time.

Makes 6 to 8 servings

Fresh Fruit Flan

½ cup (1 stick) butter at room temperature
⅓ cup sugar
½ teaspoon vanilla
1¼ cups unbleached all-purpose flour

Filling and Glaze

8 ounces cream cheese
⅓ cup sugar
1 teaspoon vanilla
An assortment of sliced fruit, such as strawberries, apricots,
    kiwis, raspberries, and blueberries, sliced as necessary
1 cup apricot jam
⅛ cup brandy (optional)

Preheat the oven to 375°F and butter a 10-inch ramekin. In a medium bowl, cream together the butter and sugar. Add the vanilla and flour and mix until crumbly. Press the dough into the prepared ramekin and bake in the preheated oven for 15 to 20 minutes, or until golden brown. Place on a rack to cool.

To make the filling: Beat together the cream cheese, sugar, and vanilla until well blended. Spread this mixture over the cooled pastry shell. Arrange the fresh fruit decoratively on top.

In the top of a double boiler, heat the apricot jam over simmering water, until completely melted. Add the brandy if the jam is too thick to spread. Using a pastry brush, brush the top of the fruit with the apricot glaze, being sure to coat all the surfaces. Chill in the refrigerator for 2 to 4 hours.

Makes one 10-inch flan

Harbourfront Centre

grano Italica
Toronto, Ontario

Harbourfront Centre is a festive strand of waterfront that nurtures Toronto's thriving cultural scene by presenting free summer concerts, stage performances, dances, and art displays. Harbourfront has presented the finest in contemporary and ground-breaking jazz every summer for the past sixteen years. World Roots music is explored with performances by artists from over twenty nations in over three hundred musical experiences. An operatic weekend features the opera stars, orchestra, and chorus of the Canadian Opera Company. Harbourfront is the site of Canada's largest theater festival as well as the International Children's Film Festival.

The following picnic was created by chef Lucia Ruggiero of grano, a restaurant and bakery created by Lucia and her husband, Robert Martella. Their popular restaurant offers the kind of authentic Italian food they were both raised on. During frequent trips to Italy they check out the latest food trends, find suppliers for the restaurant, and learn more about the country of their heritage; grano Italica now includes an Italian shop that offers everything from Pavarotti recordings to Italian language lessons and sunglasses.

A Picnic at Harbourfront Centre

Potato Croquettes

Spinach Ricotta Croquettes

Caponata

Cold Trout with Orange Marinade

Biscotti di Prato

Potato Croquettes

5 or 6 baking potatoes
2 eggs
½ cup grated Parmesan cheese
Chopped fresh parsley to taste
Salt and pepper to taste
Seasoned dry bread crumbs for coating
Vegetable oil for deep frying

Peel the potatoes, dropping them into a kettle of cold salted water as you work. Bring the water to a boil and cook until the potatoes are tender but still firm, about 20 minutes. Drain the potatoes, place them in a large bowl, and mash by hand or using an electric mixer. Beat in the eggs, Parmesan, parsley, salt, and pepper.

Using the palm of your hand, roll a tablespoon of the potato mixture into an egg-shaped ball and roll in the bread crumbs; repeat with the remaining potato mixture. In a large, heavy skillet, heat about 1 inch of vegetable oil over medium-high heat until hot but not smoking. Carefully place the croquettes in the hot oil, leaving plenty of space between the pieces. Fry, turning once, until the croquettes are golden brown, about 2 minutes. Drain on paper towels and wrap in aluminum foil. Serve hot or at room temperature.

Makes 10 to 15 croquettes

Spinach Ricotta Croquettes

1 small bunch spinach, stemmed
1 pound ricotta, drained in a fine sieve
2 eggs
½ cup grated Parmesan cheese
Chopped fresh parsley, salt, and pepper to taste
Seasoned dry bread crumbs for coating
Vegetable oil for deep frying

Wash the spinach and place it, still wet, in a covered pan. Cook 3 or 4 minutes over high heat until wilted. Place in a sieve and press with the back of a large spoon to drain the excess liquid.

In a large bowl, beat the eggs; stir in the ricotta, Parmesan, parsley, salt, and pepper. Stir in the steamed spinach, mixing until the dough holds together and is well blended.

Shape the dough into egg-sized balls and roll in the bread crumbs. In a large, heavy skillet, heat about 1 inch of vegetable oil over medium-high heat until hot but not smoking. Carefully place the croquettes in the hot oil, leaving plenty of space between the pieces. Fry, turning once, until the croquettes are golden brown, about 2 minutes; do not overcook or they will fall apart. Drain on paper towels and wrap in aluminum foil. Serve hot or at room temperature.

Makes about 20 croquettes

Caponata

Caponata is an Italian ratatouille in which each vegetable is cooked separately in olive oil. It tastes even better if prepared a day in advance and stored overnight in the refrigerator.

1 eggplant, peeled and cut into 1-inch cubes
1 teaspoon salt
4 celery stalks with leaves
6 tablespoons olive oil
1 onion, diced
2 red bell peppers, cored, seeded, and cut into 1-inch squares
1 green bell pepper, cored, seeded, and cut into 1-inch squares
¼ cup capers
¼ cup red or white wine vinegar
Dash of balsamic vinegar
1 cup tomato sauce
1 tablespoon chopped basil leaves
Salt and pepper to taste

Place the eggplant in a colander, sprinkle it with the salt, and let it drain for 1 hour. Pat the eggplant dry with paper towels and set aside.

Dice the celery stalks and mince the leaves. In a large skillet or sauté pan, heat 2 tablespoons of the olive oil over medium heat and sauté the celery and onion until translucent, about 8 minutes; using a slotted spoon, remove them from the pan and set aside.

Add 2 more tablespoons of the olive oil to the same pan and sauté the peppers over medium-high heat until soft, about 10 minutes. Using a slotted spoon, remove the peppers from the pan and set aside. Add the remaining 2 tablespoons of olive oil to the pan and sauté the eggplant over medium-high heat for 10 minutes, or until softened but not completely cooked through; stir often.

In a large, heavy skillet deep enough to hold all the vegetables, combine the celery, onions, peppers, and eggplant and sauté over medium-low heat for 5 minutes. Stir in the capers, vinegars, tomato sauce, basil, salt, and pepper and continue cooking until all the vegetables are tender, about 30 minutes. Serve warm or at room temperature.

Makes 6 to 8 servings

Cold Trout with Orange Marinade

The trout should be prepared at least one day in advance and can be stored in the refrigerator for up to three days.

Three ¾-pound trout, perch, or other
   fresh-water fish, cleaned, scaled, and filleted
½ cup flour
½ cup olive oil
2 tablespoons minced onion
1 cup dry white Italian vermouth
2 tablespoons minced orange zest
½ cup freshly squeezed orange juice
Juice of one lemon
1 tablespoon salt
Freshly ground black pepper to taste
1½ tablespoons chopped parsley
Unpeeled orange slices

   Wash the trout fillets in cold water and pat dry. Sprinkle the flour on a plate and coat each trout well with it. In a large, heavy skillet, heat the olive oil over medium-high heat and fry the trout, turning once, until golden and crisp, about 10 minutes. Transfer the trout to a large, deep dish; lay them in flat, skin-side down.

   In the same skillet and hot olive oil, sauté the onions until golden, about 5 minutes. Add the vermouth and orange zest, and boil for 20 seconds. Stir in the orange juice, lemon juice, salt, and pepper, and simmer for 30 seconds, stirring constantly. Stir in the parsley. Remove from the heat and pour the hot marinade over the trout.

   Let the fish marinate at room temperature for at least 6 hours, then cover with plastic wrap and refrigerate. Serve the trout at room temperature, garnished with orange slices.

Makes 6 servings

Biscotti di Prato

6 eggs
¼ cup anisette liqueur
1 cup vegetable oil
About 2 cups flour
2 cups sugar
2 tablespoons baking powder
Pinch of salt
Zest of 1 lemon, chopped
½ cup dried fruit
½ chopped almonds

Preheat the oven to 300°F. Grease and flour a baking sheet.

In a small bowl, whisk together the eggs, anisette, and vegetable oil.

In a large bowl, combine the flour, sugar, baking powder, and salt. Add the egg mixture to the flour mixture and beat until just blended, about 1 minute. Do not overmix. Gently fold in the lemon zest, dried fruit, and almonds. Divide the dough in half.

Shape the dough into 2 logs about ½ inch thick, 1½ inches wide, and 12 inches long, patting and molding the dough with your hands. Place on the prepared baking sheet spacing the logs at least 2 inches apart.

Bake in the middle of the preheated oven for 50 minutes, or until golden brown. Transfer from the baking sheet to a rack to cool for 5 to 7 minutes. Reserve the baking sheet for finishing the cookies, below. Place the logs on a cutting board and, using a serrated knife, slice them diagonally (at a 45° angle) into ½-inch-thick biscotti.

Reduce the oven temperature to 275°F. Lay the biscotti, cut surfaces down, on the baking sheet and bake for 20 to 25 minutes, or until toasted, turning them once so that they bake evenly. Allow to cool on a rack before storing them in a tightly covered container.

Makes about 40 cookies

Hollywood Bowl Summer Festival

Hollywood, California

Engine Co. No. 38

Los Angeles, California

The Hollywood Bowl's grand summertime tradition of concerts under the stars brings Southern California the best in classical music, pops, and jazz six nights a week during an eleven-week season. Classical music lovers will hear performances by the Los Angeles Philharmonic and the Hollywood Bowl Orchestra as well as recitals by world-renowned artists. Weekends of pops showcase the music of Broadway, the silver screen, and popular favorites from the concert hall. The Bowl's jazz series presents performances by the world's outstanding jazz artists. Concertgoers often arrive early to picnic at one of thirteen beautiful picnic sites.

The following picnic was created by Ed Kasky of Engine Co. No. 28. This restaurant is located in a restored 1912 firehouse among the modern high-rises of downtown Los Angeles. The restaurant's style and decor are charmingly reminiscent of a bygone era, and its menu of traditional American classics features grilled specialties and old-fashioned desserts.

Picnic at the Hollywood Bowl

Carrot Ginger Vichyssoise

Pan-Fried Chicken

Coleslaw

Roasted Potato Salad

Rice Pudding

Engine Co. No. 38

Carrot Ginger Vichyssoise

2 tablespoons olive oil
1 garlic clove, sliced
1 inch fresh ginger root, peeled and thinly sliced
1 leek, white part only, washed well and sliced
8 medium carrots, peeled and chopped into large pieces
2 medium potatoes, peeled and chopped into large pieces
2 bay leaves
8 cups chicken stock
1 teaspoon salt
½ teaspoon freshly ground black pepper
1 cup heavy (whipping) cream or half-and-half
Chives for garnish

In a large soup kettle, heat the olive oil over low heat and sauté the garlic and ginger until soft, about 5 minutes. Raise the heat to medium, add the leek, and sauté until the leek begins to wilt, about 10 minutes. Raise the heat to high, and add the carrots, potatoes, bay leaves, chicken stock, salt, and pepper; bring to a boil. Reduce the heat to low and simmer until the vegetables are soft, about 40 minutes.

In a blender or food processor, purée the soup in batches. Return to the kettle and stir in the cream or half-and-half; add more salt and pepper if needed. Pour the soup into a storage container and cool to room temperature before refrigerating. Serve in chilled soup bowls and garnish with snipped chives.

Makes 8 servings

Engine Co. No. 38

Pan-Fried Chicken

6 chicken breast halves, boned
6 chicken thighs, boned
1 tablespoon salt
1 tablespoon black pepper
2 cups buttermilk
1½ to 2 cups unbleached all-purpose flour
Peanut oil for frying

Rinse the chicken pieces well, pat dry, and place in a large, shallow dish. Sprinkle the chicken with half the salt and pepper, and cover with the buttermilk. Cover with plastic wrap and refrigerate for at least 6 hours, or overnight.

In another shallow dish, combine the remaining salt and pepper with the flour. Drain the buttermilk from the chicken pieces, but do not dry them. Dredge the chicken in the flour mixture and place the pieces in a single layer on a platter.

Preheat the oven to 400°F. In a large, heavy skillet, add the oil to a depth of about 1 inch and heat until hot but not smoking. Carefully place the chicken in the hot oil, leaving plenty of space between the pieces. Fry, turning once, until the chicken is golden brown. Transfer to a baking pan and bake in the preheated oven until the juices run clear, about 10 minutes or until a meat thermometer inserted into the center of each piece reads 160°F. Cool the chicken on paper towels, and refrigerate until ready to pack the picnic.

Makes 6 servings

Coleslaw

This zesty salad is easy to prepare. The dressing can be prepared a few days in advance and kept refrigerated.

1 cup mayonnaise
¼ cup buttermilk
3 tablespoons white wine vinegar
½ tablespoon sugar
1½ tablespoons prepared horseradish
1½ tablespoons fresh lemon juice
¾ teaspoon salt
½ teaspoon white pepper
3 cups shredded green cabbage
1 cup shredded red cabbage
1 cup red onion, sliced very thin

In a large bowl, whisk together all the ingredients except the cabbage and onion. Refrigerate if made ahead. The day of the picnic, add the cabbage and onion and toss to coat with the dressing. Refrigerate until time to pack for the picnic.

Makes 6 to 8 servings

Roasted Potato Salad

Serve this salad warm or at room temperature the same day, because it does not keep well. If a spicier salad is desired, add some cayenne pepper.

¼ cup olive oil
2 pounds red new potatoes, washed and quartered
1 teaspoon salt
½ cup red bell pepper, cored, seeded, and diced
1 ½ tablespoons minced shallot
1 teaspoon minced fresh thyme
1 teaspoon minced fresh rosemary
1 teaspoon freshly ground black pepper
1 teaspoon paprika
½ teaspoon granulated garlic or 1 teaspoon minced garlic
1 teaspoon fresh lemon juice
1 tablespoon parsley, chopped

Preheat the oven to 400°F. In a heavy, ovenproof skillet, heat the olive oil over medium heat and add the potatoes. Sprinkle with salt and toss to coat evenly with the olive oil. Place the pan in the oven and bake until the potatoes are slightly soft, about 20 minutes. Remove from the oven; add the bell pepper, shallot, thyme, rosemary, black pepper, paprika, and garlic. Toss to combine all the ingredients. Return the pan to the oven and bake until the potatoes are soft when pierced with a sharp knife, about 10 to 15 minutes.

Remove the pan from the oven. Using a slotted spoon, transfer the ingredients to a medium bowl and toss with the lemon juice and parsley. Season with more salt and pepper if necessary.

Makes 6 servings

Rice Pudding

1 cup medium-grain white rice
1½ cups water
½ teaspoon salt
3 cups milk
1 cinnamon stick
1 vanilla bean, split and scraped, or 1 teaspoon vanilla extract
⅔ cup sugar
⅓ cup golden raisins
⅓ cup red flame raisins
3 tablespoons heavy (whipping) cream
1 egg yolk
Ground cinnamon for sprinkling

Combine the rice, water, and salt in a heavy-bottomed saucepan over medium heat and simmer until the water evaporates. Add the milk, cinnamon stick, and vanilla bean, if using. Reduce to low heat and continue to cook, stirring every 2 or 3 minutes. Remove from the heat before all the milk is absorbed, when the rice is still slightly runny. Discard the vanilla bean and add the sugar and raisins. Let cool ½ hour, stirring occasionally. Add the cream, egg yolk, and vanilla extract, if using. Allow the pudding to cool to room temperature and sprinkle with cinnamon. When completely cooled, place in the refrigerator and chill until time to pack for the picnic.

Makes 6 to 8 servings

Engine Co. No. 38

Interlochen Arts Festival

Interlochen, Michigan

The Embers on the Bay

Acme, Michigan

The Interlochen Center for the Arts is a permanent training center for young musicians, dancers, actors, visual artists, and writers. A nonprofit organization, the center has three component programs: Interlochen Arts Academy, an outgrowth of the National Music Camp, Interlochen Arts Camp and Interlochen Public Radio. The Interlochen Arts Festival draws on the talents of these programs. Throughout the summer, the festival presents more than 750 programs of chamber music, orchestral works, instrumental and vocal recitals, opera, jazz, pops, band music, drama, and dance in a wooded sanctuary in northern Michigan. Performers include students, faculty, staff, and world-renowned classical, pop, and jazz guest artists.

The following picnic was created by Keith Charters, owner and chef of The Embers on the Bay. "Picnics under the Pines," catered by The Embers, offers Interlochen concertgoers delectable picnics before festival concerts.

Picnic at Interlochen

Cajun Shrimp and Andouille Sausage Kebabs

Tailgate Potato Salad

*Grilled Spiced Pork Tenderloin with
Honey Jalapeño Sauce*

Fresh Stuffed Corn

Fresh Pears with Blueberry Cream

The Embers on the Bay

Cajun Shrimp and Andouille Sausage Kebabs

4 wooden skewers, soaked overnight in water
1 pound jumbo shrimp with tails, shelled and deveined
1 pound smoked andouille sausage, cut into 1½-inch slices
Marinade (recipe follows)

Place a wooden skewer through the tail end of a shrimp and then through a sausage; skewer the top of the shrimp over the sausage. Each skewer should contain four pieces of shrimp and four slices of sausage. Place the kebabs in a shallow dish and pour the marinade over; it should cover the kebabs. Cover with plastic wrap and marinate in the refrigerator overnight.

Light a charcoal fire in an open grill. Grill the kebabs over a hot fire, turning after about 3 minutes. Grill 3 minutes on the second side, remove from the grill, and wrap in aluminum foil.

Makes 4 servings

Marinade

4 ounces (1 stick) unsalted butter
¾ teaspoon minced garlic
¼ teaspoon cayenne pepper
¼ teaspoon freshly ground black pepper
¼ teaspoon crushed red pepper
¼ teaspoon ground thyme
¼ teaspoon ground rosemary
¼ teaspoon salt
¼ cup beer
1 teaspoon Worcestershire sauce

½ cup shrimp stock or chicken broth
¼ cup pale dry sherry

   In a small saucepan, melt the butter over medium heat and sauté the garlic until soft. Add the rest of the ingredients and simmer until the liquid has reduced to three quarters of the original volume.

Tailgate Potato Salad

1 cup green beans, trimmed and cut into 1-inch pieces
1 pound new red potatoes
Vinaigrette (recipe follows)
¾ cup crumbled feta cheese
¾ cup sliced ripe olives
½ cup sliced green onions
¼ cup finely diced green bell pepper
¾ cup sliced red radishes
Lettuce leaves for garnish

Bring a saucepan of water to a boil and add the green beans. Simmer until the beans are just tender, about 4 or 5 minutes. Drain, rinse under cold water, and drain again. Pat dry with paper towels and set aside.

Peel the potatoes, dropping them into a kettle of cold salted water as you work. Bring the water to a boil and cook until the potatoes are tender but still firm, about 20 minutes. Drain the potatoes, quarter them, and place in a large bowl. Sprinkle the still-warm potatoes with the vinaigrette. Add the feta cheese, olives, green onions, bell pepper, and radishes; toss gently to combine. Cool to room temperature, cover with plastic wrap, and refrigerate overnight. Serve at the picnic on a bed of lettuce.

Makes 4 servings

Vinaigrette

½ cup extra-virgin olive oil
¼ cup white wine vinegar
1 teaspoon salt
Freshly ground black pepper to taste

In a small bowl, whisk together all the ingredients until emulsified.

The Embers on the Bay

Grilled Spiced Pork Tenderloin with Honey Jalapeño Sauce

½ cup brown sugar
1½ tablespoons salt
1 tablespoon dried thyme
½ tablespoon ground cumin
1 tablespoon crushed bay leaf
1 teaspoon freshly ground black pepper
1 teaspoon ground oregano
½ teaspoon ground allspice
¼ teaspoon ground cloves
¼ teaspoon ground cinnamon
1 tablespoon ground cardamom
2 pounds pork tenderloin, trimmed of silver skin
Basting Sauce (recipe follows)
Honey Jalapeño Sauce (recipe follows)

In a large shallow dish, mix together all the ingredients except the pork tenderloins. Add the tenderloin and coat completely. Cover with plastic wrap and marinate overnight in the refrigerator.

Light a charcoal fire in an open grill. Grill the tenderloin over the hot fire, turning and basting with the basting sauce every 3 minutes. Grill for a total of 20 minutes. Slice the meat thinly on the bias when slightly cool and arrange on a platter. Refrigerate until the picnic. Serve with honey jalapeño sauce.

Makes 4 servings

Basting Sauce

1 cup apple cider
3 tablespoons brown sugar
2 tablespoons chili powder

In a small bowl, whisk together all the ingredients.

Honey Jalapeño Sauce

2 jalapeño peppers, seeded
¼ cup honey
1 tablespoon minced garlic
1 tablespoon minced fresh cilantro
½ teaspoon allspice
½ teaspoon cumin
2 teaspoons olive oil
2 teaspoons balsamic vinegar
2 teaspoons Dijon mustard

In a blender or food processor, process all the ingredients until smooth and transfer to a small container for transport.

Fresh Stuffed Corn

4 ears of corn, with husks
6 ounces unsalted butter
1 red onion, cut in ¼-inch dice
8 ounces sliced fresh mushrooms
1 red bell pepper, cut in ¼-inch dice
1 green bell pepper, cut in ¼-inch dice
1½ teaspoons salt
¼ teaspoon white pepper
1 teaspoon Tabasco sauce
4 ounces heavy (whipping) cream
4 ounces Monterey jack cheese, sliced

Preheat the oven to 350°F. Shuck the top third of each corn husk. Make an incision in the bottom of the ear of corn, leaving about ¼ inch on the bottom, and pop the ear of corn out of the husk. Clean the inside of the husk of all silk strands and wash. Remove strands from the ears of corn as well. Cut the corn kernels off the cobs.

In a sauté pan, melt the butter over medium heat and sauté the onions until translucent, about 5 minutes. Add the corn kernels and mushrooms, and sauté for 3 minutes. Add the bell peppers, salt, pepper, and Tabasco sauce. Simmer for 3 minutes, or until the corn is tender. Add the cream. Spoon the corn mixture back into the cleaned corn husks and transfer to a baking sheet. Place the cheese slices on top and bake in the preheated oven until the cheese melts. Serve at room temperature.

Makes 4 servings

The Embers on the Bay

Fresh Pears with Blueberry Cream

½ cup vanilla yogurt
¼ cup honey
½ cup fresh blueberries, washed and drained
4 Anjou pears

In a medium bowl, stir together the yogurt, honey, and blueberries. Peel, core, and thinly slice the pears, leaving the stem intact if possible. Fan the pear slices out on each of 4 plates and spoon over a little blueberry cream.

Makes 4 servings

International Carillon Festival
Springfield, Illinois

Janet Rogers
Rochester, Illinois

The International Carillon Festival hosts international carillonneurs during week-long festivities in June. Concerts are performed on the Rees Memorial Carillon, one of the finest and largest carillons in the world. Its open tower has 66 cast-bronze bells that range in weight from 22 pounds to 7½ tons. The bells are played manually on a keyboard located in the carillonneur's cabin. For the past fifteen years, carillonneur Karel Keldermans has organized the festival.

Classical programs of music written especially for the carillon, transcribed pieces, folk, and popular tunes are performed at the festival. Concerts are best heard from a distance of more than 300 feet, and the lawn west of the tower or the Rose Garden in Washington Park are excellent places from which to listen while enjoying a picnic.

The following picnic was created by Janet W. Rogers, food service director of the First United Methodist Church in Springfield and a caterer especially noted for decorated cakes and wedding cakes.

Picnic at the Carillon International Music Festival

Crabby Eggs

Turkey Pecan Croissants

Salad Supreme

Gooey Butter Cake

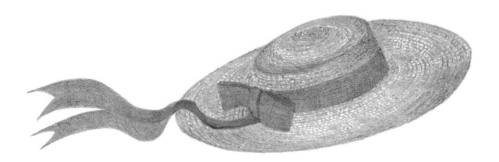

Janet Rogers

Crabby Eggs

Hard-cooked eggs will keep in the refrigerator submerged in water in an uncovered container for two to three days.

6 eggs
6 ounces shredded crabmeat
3 tablespoons mayonnaise
1 teaspoon Worcestershire sauce
⅛ teaspoon Tabasco sauce
Fresh dill for garnish

Place the eggs in a medium pot and cover with cold water an inch above the tops of the eggs. Bring the water to a boil over high heat, then reduce the heat to low and simmer for 12 minutes. Place the eggs under cold water, crack the shells, peel the eggs, and run them under cool water again. Slice the eggs in half lengthwise and carefully remove the yolks.

In a medium bowl, mash the egg yolks and combine with the shredded crabmeat. Stir in the mayonnaise, Worcestershire sauce, and Tabasco sauce. Spoon this mixture into the egg whites, or use a pastry tube to pipe the mixture into the egg whites. Garnish the tops with dill and arrange the eggs in a single layer in a container. Cover with plastic wrap and refrigerate until ready to pack for the picnic.

Makes 6 servings

Turkey Pecan Croissants

4 tablespoons (½ stick) butter at room temperature
½ cup finely chopped pecans
1½ teaspoons grated orange zest
4 croissants, sliced in half
4 ounces cooked turkey breast, thinly sliced
Lettuce leaves

In a medium bowl, combine the butter, pecans, and orange zest, and mix until well blended. Spread this mixture onto half of each croissant, top with slices of turkey and lettuce, and cover with the other croissant half.

Makes 8 servings

Salad Supreme

½ cup olive oil
⅓ cup red wine vinegar
2 tablespoons sugar
½ cup grated Parmesan cheese
1 head red or green leaf lettuce, torn into bite-sized pieces
One 6-ounce jar artichoke hearts, drained and quartered
One 3-ounce can black olives
One 14-ounce can hearts of palm, drained and sliced (optional)

In a small bowl, whisk together the olive oil, vinegar, sugar, and Parmesan cheese.

In a large bowl, combine the lettuce, artichoke hearts, olives, and hearts of palm. Just before serving, toss with the vinaigrette.

Makes 4 to 6 servings

Gooey Butter Cake

3 cups cake flour
1¾ cups sugar
⅓ cup powdered milk
2 ½ teaspoons baking powder
1 teaspoon salt
1 cup plus 2 tablespoons butter, melted
2 eggs
1½ teaspoons vanilla

Topping

8 ounces cream cheese at room temperature
2 eggs
1 teaspoon vanilla
1 pound powdered sugar

Preheat the oven to 350°F. Butter and flour a 16-by-11-inch jelly roll pan.

In a large bowl, sift together the flour, sugar, powdered milk, baking powder, and salt. Beat in the melted butter, eggs, and vanilla, beating until the batter is smooth. Spread into the prepared pan.

To make the topping: In a medium bowl, beat the cream cheese until fluffy. Add the eggs, vanilla, and powdered sugar and beat until smooth. Spread the topping evenly over the cake batter. Bake in the preheated oven for 25 to 30 minutes, or until a toothpick inserted in the center of the cake comes out clean. Cool and cut into 2-inch squares.

Makes one 16-by-11-inch cake

Festival International de Lanaudière
Joliette, Québec

Auberge Ripplecove Inn
Ayer's Cliff, Québec

The Festival International de Lanaudière offers over forty classical music performances from late June to the end of July in a beautiful countryside setting only fifty miles from Montréal. Prominent national and international artists perform in the festival amphitheater, which seats ten thousand and has exceptional acoustics. Another dozen festival concerts are held in the magnificently preserved churches of the Lanaudière region. The festival's programming includes opera, symphony orchestra, and dance performances, as well as concerts for the whole family on Sunday afternoons.

The following picnic was created by the Auberge Ripplecove Inn, a resort on the shores of Lake Massawippi. The inn has received the Four Diamond Award from the American Automobile Association since 1988, and its dining room was awarded Quebec's highest "four fork" rating by the Ministry of Tourism. Auberge Ripplecove is a member of the European Relais du Silence.

Picnic at the Festival International de Lanaudière

Cold Avocado Soup with Diced Red Peppers

*Salmon Terrine with Pink Shrimp and
Watercress Coulis*

*Spinach Salad with Poached Quail Eggs, Smoked Trout,
and Pistachio Vinaigrette*

Citrus Salad with Kiwi Coulis

Auberge Ripplecove Inn

Cold Avocado Soup with Diced Red Peppers

6 ripe avocados, pitted and peeled
2 cups chicken stock or broth
1 garlic clove, minced
Salt and white pepper to taste
1 cup half and half
1 red bell pepper, cored, seeded, and diced (optional)

In a large bowl, coarsely chop the avocados. Add the chicken stock or broth, garlic, salt, and pepper; mix well. Stir in the cream. Transfer to a food processor and process until fairly smooth; a bit of texture should remain. Transfer to a bowl and chill in the refrigerator for at least 2 hours.

To serve, divide the soup among serving bowls or cups; sprinkle with the diced red peppers if desired.

Makes 8 servings

Auberge Ripplecove Inn

Salmon Terrine with Pink Shrimp and Watercress Coulis

1 pound poached salmon, flaked
4 egg whites
Salt and white pepper to taste
Cayenne pepper to taste
1 cup heavy (whipping) cream
3 or 4 ounces pink shrimp, coarsely chopped
2 bunches watercress
½ cup chicken stock or broth

Preheat the oven to 350°F and butter a terrine. In a medium bowl, stir together the flaked salmon, egg whites, salt, white pepper, and cayenne. Fold in the cream and shrimp. Transfer the mixture to a terrine and cover with a double thickness of aluminum foil. Place the terrine in a larger pan and fill the pan with enough hot water to reach halfway up the sides of the terrine. Bake in the preheated oven for 60 minutes, or until the top feels slightly springy and is beginning to shrink away from the sides of the mold. Cool to room temperature, cover with plastic wrap, and chill in the refrigerator.

To make the watercress coulis: In a food processor, purée the watercress and chicken stock or broth. To serve, unmold the terrine, pour some of the coulis on each plate, and top with slices of the salmon terrine.

Makes 4 to 6 servings

Spinach Salad with Poached Quail Eggs, Smoked Trout, and Pistachio Vinaigrette

2½ tablespoons white vinegar
8 quail eggs
Pistachio Vinaigrette (recipe follows)
1 pound spinach, rinsed and patted dry
½ pound smoked trout, sliced

Add the vinegar to a quart of boiling water. Break the quail eggs into the water and lower the heat to medium. Poach the eggs in barely simmering water for 2 minutes. Carefully remove with a slotted spoon and chill in the refrigerator.

To serve, toss together the spinach and pistachio vinaigrette, reserving a little vinaigrette for the trout and quail eggs. Arrange the spinach salad on 4 plates and top with the slices of smoked trout and poached quail eggs. Spoon over some of the remaining vinaigrette.

Makes 4 servings

Pistachio Vinaigrette

⅓ cup champagne vinegar
Salt and freshly ground black pepper to taste
1 cup olive oil
¾ cup pistachios, shelled and chopped

In a small bowl, whisk together the vinegar, salt, pepper, and olive oil. Stir in the pistachios.

Auberge Ripplecove Inn

Citrus Salad with Kiwi Coulis

3 tablespoons sugar
3 tablespoons water
1 white grapefruit
1 pink grapefruit
1 orange
1 blood orange
1 tangerine
½ lemon
½ lime
2 tablespoons Kirsch
6 kiwis, peeled

In a small saucepan, bring the sugar and water to a boil, cook over high heat stirring until the liquid reaches the consistency of a syrup; remove from the heat and let cool.

Peel the grapefruit, orange, tangerine, lemon, and lime removing all pith; slice thinly.

In a large bowl, combine the fruit, half of the syrup, and the kirsch and mix thoroughly. Cover with plastic wrap and refrigerate for a few hours.

In a food processor, purée the kiwis and the remaining syrup. Transfer to a small covered container and chill until ready to pack for the picnic. To serve, pour some of the kiwi coulis on each plate and top with the citrus.

Makes 8 servings

New York Philharmonic Free Parks Concerts

Balducci's
New York, New York

More than eleven million people have attended the New York Philharmonic Free Parks Concerts since they began in 1965, with many audiences numbering more than 150,000. The Philharmonic concerts take place in several locations in Suffolk and Westchester counties and in the five boroughs of New York. Avid music lovers enjoy programs of familiar orchestral works with world-renowned soloists and guest conductors. Picnics are a major part of this popular summer ritual.

The following picnic was created by Richard Tarlov of Balducci's. For three quarters of a century Balducci's has been a favorite family-owned grocer in Greenwich Village and is now known to connoisseurs as one of the world's leading fine-food establishments. The store is devoted solely to food, and each of its many departments is a minimarket unto itself. Services include personal shopping, catering, and gift baskets.

Picnic at the New York Philharmonic's Free Parks Concerts

Nina's Grilled Marinated Quail

Fresh Tomato Salad

Orecchiette with Asparagus

Fresh Fruit Skewers with Honey-Mint Dressing

Nina's Grilled Marinated Quail

A brush of fresh parsley, thyme, and oregano tied with twine may be used for basting and will make an attractive garnish for the center of the serving platter.

¼ cup brandy
¼ cup Madeira
2 teaspoons minced garlic
¼ teaspoon salt
¼ teaspoon freshly ground black pepper
6 fresh sage leaves, chopped
6 small sprigs rosemary, chopped
6 sprigs thyme, chopped
4 quail, butterflied

In a small glass baking dish, mix together all the ingredients except the quail. Place the quail in the marinade, cover with plastic wrap, and refrigerate overnight, turning once or twice.

Light a charcoal fire in an open grill. When the coals are white-hot, remove the quail from the marinade and grill, skin side down, for 2 minutes, basting with the marinade. Turn and grill for 2 or 3 minutes more. Place on a serving platter, cover with plastic wrap, and pack with the cold food for the picnic.

Makes 2 servings

Fresh Tomato Salad

4 garden-fresh tomatoes
Extra-virgin olive oil for drizzling
Balsamic vinegar for sprinkling
Chopped basil for sprinkling

Cut the tomatoes in thick slices and arrange them on a plate. Drizzle over the olive oil and sprinkle with vinegar and basil.

Makes 4 to 6 servings

Orecchiette with Asparagus Tips

Orecchiette are specially shaped pasta resembling "little ears."

¼ cup sherry vinegar
1 teaspoon Dijon mustard
½ teaspoon salt
Freshly ground black pepper to taste
1 clove garlic, minced
½ cup extra-virgin olive oil
½ pound asparagus
1 tablespoon sugar
½ pound dried orecchiette
1 tablespoon chopped Italian parsley

In a small bowl, stir together the vinegar, mustard, salt, pepper, and garlic. Gradually whisk in the olive oil until the dressing emulsifies; set aside.

Cut the tender part of each asparagus stalk on the diagonal into 1-inch pieces. Bring 1 quart of water to a boil and add the sugar, this keeps the vegetables bright green. Add the asparagus pieces and cook for 3 or 4 minutes until crisp-tender; run under cold water, drain, and set aside.

Bring 6 cups of salted water to a boil and cook the orecchiette for 8 to 10 minutes, or until *al dente;* drain.

In a large bowl, combine the asparagus and orecchiette. If the salad will be eaten within half an hour, toss with the sherry vinaigrette. Add the parsley at the end. If the pasta will be in transit to the picnic site any longer than that, drizzle on a little olive oil when first combining the asparagus and orecchiette. Bring the sherry vinaigrette along in a separate container. Toss with the vinaigrette a half hour before serving, adding the parsley last.

Makes 4 servings

Fresh Fruit Skewers with Honey-Mint Dressing

Accompany this light fruit dessert with madeleines and pignoli cookies.

An assortment of melon balls, strawberries, pineapple chunks, kiwi slices
1 pint heavy (whipping) cream
3 tablespoons honey
2 tablespoons fresh chopped mint

Skewer the melon balls, strawberries, pineapple chunks, and slices of kiwi on wooden skewers. In a small container, whisk or shake together the cream, honey, and mint. Arrange the skewers on a plate, cover with plastic wrap, and pack with the cold foods for the picnic. Dip the fruit skewers into the dressing at the picnic.

Makes 4 to 6 servings

Newport Music Festival
JVC Jazz Festival

Kathleen's Fantastic Food & Catering
Newport, Rhode Island

In a setting of phenomenal splendor by the sea, the Newport Music Festival continues its tradition of presenting chamber music, recitals by world-class artists, American debuts by important pianists, and special events in the fabled mansions of Newport. To create an extraordinary festival, General Director Mark P. Malkovich III researches and selects works from the nineteenth-century chamber music and vocal repertoires and from the piano literature of the Romantic era. Dozens of world premieres of contemporary composers as well as rare discoveries of forgotten minor masterpieces have delighted festival audiences. Each season for two weeks in July, more than forty-five concerts are performed by outstanding musicians from around the world. Most of the formal evening concerts are held in the Great Hall of the Breakers while the morning and afternoon concerts take place in stately homes turned into elegant concert halls.

For three days in August, Newport's JVC Jazz Festival is noted for assembling the world's greatest jazz artists. A list of performers in the past and recent seasons is virtually a history of jazz and a foreshowing of future stars. Concerts by vocal and instrumental soloists, big bands, and combos are held at the Newport Casino in the International Tennis Hall of Fame. Outdoor concerts are held in Fort Adams State Park on a huge lawn overlooking beautiful Narragansett Bay. Everyone is encouraged to picnic, relax, and enjoy the atmosphere.

The following picnic was created by Kathleen Geasey of Kathleen's Fantastic Food and Catering. A retired ballet dancer, Kathleen now makes a second career of catering and running two food stores with her husband, William Geasey. Kathleen's cuisine is noted for delicious variety with influences from many regions including China, France, Thailand, New Orleans, and New England.

Picnic by Narragansett Bay

Scandinavian Cucumber Salad

Indonesian Sesame Noodle Salad

*Mandarin Tenderloin Salad with
Poppyseed Dressing*

Southern Pecan Squares

*Fresh Strawberries with
Brown Sugar and Crème Fraîche*

Kathleen's Fantastic Food & Catering

Scandinavian Cucumber Salad

4 cucumbers, peeled
2 teaspoons salt
1 onion, thinly sliced
½ cup white wine vinegar
2 teaspoons paprika
1 teaspoon sugar

Slice the cucumbers as thinly as possible; put them in a large bowl. Sprinkle with salt, cover with plastic wrap, and refrigerate overnight. Drain the cucumbers well over a fine sieve. In a medium bowl, combine the onion slices, vinegar, paprika, and sugar, and stir in the cucumber slices. Cover and chill thoroughly in the refrigerator.

Makes 6 servings

Kathleen's Fantastic Food & Catering

Indonesian Sesame Noodle Salad

1½ tablespoons vegetable oil

3 green onions, minced

3 cloves garlic, minced

1 tablespoon minced fresh ginger

3 teaspoons rice wine vinegar

3½ tablespoons soy sauce

1 tablespoon sugar

1 tablespoon tahini

½ cup chicken stock or broth

1 teaspoon sesame oil

8 ounces sesame noodles

1 red bell pepper, cored, seeded, and thinly sliced, for garnish

In a small saucepan, heat the vegetable oil over medium heat, and sauté the onion, garlic, and ginger until the onion is translucent, about 5 minutes. Add the vinegar, soy sauce, sugar, tahini, chicken stock or broth, and sesame oil. Simmer for 2 minutes, remove from the heat, and let cool.

In a large pot, bring 3 quarts of water to a boil. Add the sesame noodles and cook for 2 or 3 minutes, or until tender. Drain, run under cold water, and drain again. In a large bowl, toss together the sauce and the noodles. Serve at room temperature garnished with the red pepper slices.

Makes 4 servings

Mandarin Tenderloin Salad with Poppyseed Dressing

⅓ cup soy sauce
⅓ cup honey
⅓ cup pineapple juice
1 clove garlic, minced
1 teaspoon minced fresh ginger root
3 pounds beef tenderloin
12 oranges, sectioned
2 red onions, thinly sliced
2 red bell peppers, cored, seeded, and julienned
Lettuce and 6 chopped green onions for garnish
Poppyseed Dressing (recipe follows)

In a large nonaluminum dish, whisk together the soy sauce, honey, pineapple juice, garlic, and ginger. Add the beef tenderloin, cover, and marinate overnight in the refrigerator, turning once or twice. Broil the tenderloin until medium rare. Chill and slice thinly.

In a large bowl, toss together the sliced tenderloin, oranges, red onions, and red peppers until well combined. Line a large platter or individual serving plates with lettuce. Arrange the salad on top of the lettuce and sprinkle with the green onions. Drizzle over the poppyseed dressing.

Makes 12 servings

Poppyseed Dressing

¾ cup sugar
1 teaspoon dry mustard
1 teaspoon salt
⅓ cup cider vinegar
2 tablespoons minced onion
1 cup vegetable oil
1½ tablespoons poppyseeds

In a food processor, process the sugar, mustard, salt, vinegar, and onion until well combined. With the motor running, gradually add the vegetable oil in a thin stream until the mixture emulsifies. Stir in the poppy seeds.

Kathleen's Fantastic Food & Catering

Southern Pecan Squares

2 cups unbleached all-purpose flour
½ cup sugar
1 teaspoon baking powder
½ teaspoon salt
1 cup (2 sticks) cold butter plus ½ cup melted butter
4 eggs
2 cups light brown sugar
2 teaspoons vanilla
2 cups chopped pecans

Preheat the oven to 350°F. Butter a 9-by-13-inch baking pan. In a food processor, process the flour, sugar, baking powder, salt, and cold butter just until the mixture resembles coarse crumbs. Press the dough into the prepared pan and bake for 10 to 15 minutes, or until the crust is lightly browned.

In a medium bowl, beat together the eggs, brown sugar, melted butter, and vanilla. Fold in the pecans. Pour this mixture over the crust and return the pan to the oven for 20 to 25 minutes, or until the topping is puffy, golden, and almost set in the center. Let cool and cut into squares.

Makes about 3 dozen squares

Opera Theatre of Saint Louis

Ces & Judy's Catering
St. Louis, Missouri

The Opera Theatre of Saint Louis is noted for adventuresome programming, imaginative productions, and performances by rising young singers working with experienced conductors and directors. The operas are sung in English and are accompanied by members of the St. Louis Symphony Orchestra. Performances take place from late May to the end of June in the Loretto-Hilton Center on the campus of Webster University located in suburban St. Louis. Before the operas, festival guests enjoy relaxed preopera picnics at the campus pavilion or in a lovely setting on the lawn.

The following picnic was created by Cecily Hoffius and Judy Bellos. Their company, Ces & Judy's Catering, was founded in 1981 and provides St. Louis with fresh, creative food served with exceptional care. They are the exclusive food and beverage service for the Opera Theatre of Saint Louis.

Picnic at the Opera Theatre of Saint Louis

*Dried Cherry and Pistachio Stuffed Chicken with
Honey Mustard Sauce*

*Barbecued Pork Tenderloin with
Spicy Barbecue Sauce*

Roasted Vegetables

Potato Salad with Cucumbers and Red Onion

Lemon Curd Tartlets with Fresh Fruit

Dried Cherry and Pistachio Stuffed Chicken with Honey Mustard Sauce

2 whole chicken breasts, boned and skinned
⅓ cup dry red wine
¼ cup sugar
½ cup dried cherries
¼ cup shelled pistachio nuts
2 tablespoons olive oil
Honey Mustard Sauce (recipe follows)

Cut each chicken breast in half along the breastbone line; set aside.

In a small bowl, stir together the wine, sugar, and cherries. Let sit at room temperature until the cherries are plump, about 1 hour. Drain.

Preheat the oven to 350°F. Using a sharp knife, cut a slit in each breast to form a pocket. Lift the flap of the pocket and fill it with the cherries and pistachio nuts, making sure that none of the filling seeps out. Place the chicken breasts on a lightly oiled baking pan, brush the chicken with olive oil, and bake in the preheated oven until cooked through, about 25 to 30 minutes. Let cool and refrigerate until time to pack for the picnic. To serve, slice each chicken breast crosswise in ½-inch slices, and place in a fan shape on each plate. Spoon over some honey mustard sauce.

Makes 4 servings

Honey Mustard Sauce

1 cup sour cream
2½ tablespoons honey
1 tablespoon Dijon mustard

In a small bowl, stir together all the ingredients. Chill in the refrigerator until ready to pack for the picnic.

Ces & Judy's Catering

Barbecued Pork Tenderloin with
Spicy Barbecue Sauce

Relish

¼ cup butter
½ onion, finely chopped
½ teaspoon dry mustard
¼ teaspoon cayenne pepper
½ teaspoon paprika
1 tablespoon sugar
1 teaspoon salt
½ tablespoon Worcestershire sauce
½ tablespoon Tabasco sauce
½ tablespoon chili powder
Freshly ground black pepper to taste
1 tablespoon fresh lemon juice
¼ cup vinegar
¾ cup water
1 garlic cloves, minced

2½ pounds boneless pork tenderloin

In a sauté pan or skillet, melt the butter and sauté the onion until translucent, about 5 minutes. Stir in all the remaining ingredients except the pork and simmer over medium-low heat for 20 minutes, or until the mixture thickens. Set aside about ½ cup of the sauce for garnishing the cooked pork.

Light a charcoal fire in an open grill. Brush the pork with the remaining sauce, reserving some for basting. Grill over the hot coals for about 20 minutes, brushing with sauce as the meat cooks. Remove from the grill and let rest for 5 minutes. Cut into ½-inch slices and arrange on a serving plate. Pour over the reserved barbecue sauce.

Makes 6 servings

Ces & Judy's Catering

Roasted Vegetables

These vegetables are wonderful as a topping for pita bread, sprinkled with mozzarella cheese and heated under a broiler.

1 eggplant, cut into ½-inch cubes
2 zucchini, cut into 1-inch cubes
2 yellow squash, cut into 1-inch cubes
1 red pepper, cored, seeded, and chopped
1 yellow pepper, cored, seeded, and chopped
1 tablespoon salt
1 tablespoon freshly ground black pepper
1 teaspoon granulated garlic
1 teaspoon dried oregano
1 teaspoon dried basil
½ cup olive oil
3 tomatoes, cored and chopped

Preheat the oven to 375°F. In a large bowl, combine the eggplant, zucchini, yellow squash, and red and yellow peppers. In a small bowl, stir together the salt, pepper, garlic, oregano, and basil. Pour the spices over the vegetables and toss. Pour over the olive oil and toss to mix well. Stir in the tomatoes. Spread the vegetables on a jelly roll pan and bake in the preheated oven for 45 minutes to 1 hour, or until the vegetables are completely soft. Transfer to a colander and drain the vegetables of the excess oil. Serve hot or cold.

Makes 8 to 10 servings

Potato Salad with Cucumbers and Red Onions

This salad is best used immediately and not refrigerated. If it must be refrigerated, add the cucumbers just before serving.

3 pounds new red potatoes, peeled and cut into quarters
1 cup mayonnaise
¼ cup sour cream
¼ cup chopped fresh chives
1 teaspoon salt
Freshly ground black pepper to taste
2 cups thinly sliced, peeled cucumbers
1 cup thinly sliced red onions

In a large pot of boiling salted water, cook the potatoes until tender when pierced with a knife; drain.

In a large bowl, combine the mayonnaise, sour cream, chives, salt, and pepper, mixing well. Cut the warm potatoes into ½-inch cubes and add to the dressing. Fold in the cucumbers and onions, and toss gently.

Makes 6 servings

Lemon Curd Tartlets with Fresh Fruit

1 cup (2 sticks) butter
¼ cup sugar
1 egg
1 egg yolk
2½ cups unbleached all-purpose flour

Filling

2 eggs
5 egg yolks
1 cup sugar
1 tablespoon grated lemon zest
⅔ cup fresh lemon juice
1 tablespoon dry white wine
1 tablespoon butter
Blueberries, raspberries, or blackberries for garnish

In the large bowl of an electric mixer, cream together the butter and sugar until fluffy. Beat in the egg and egg yolk. Gradually add the flour at low speed until just incorporated; do not overmix. Form the dough into a ball, wrap in plastic wrap, and chill in the refrigerator for at least 1 hour.

On a flat surface, roll out the dough to a thickness of ⅛ inch and cut out rounds to fit six 4-inch tartlet pans. Press the dough into the bottom and sides of the tartlet pans and chill for 30 minutes.

Preheat the oven to 400°F. Prick the bottom and sides of the pastry with a fork. Line the tartlet shells with aluminum foil and fill with dried beans. Transfer to a baking sheet and bake the shells in the preheated oven for 15 minutes. Remove the foil and beans, lower the oven temperature to 350°F, and bake for 10 minutes longer, or until the edges are golden brown. Let cool and carefully

Ces & Judy's Catering

remove the pastry from the pans.

To make the filling: In a medium bowl, whisk together the eggs and egg yolks. Add the sugar, lemon zest, lemon juice, and wine, whisking until thoroughly blended. Transfer to the top of a double boiler and cook over simmering water for 5 to 7 minutes, stirring constantly until thickened. Remove from the heat, fold in the butter, and whisk to combine. Let cool to room temperature.

To assemble, spoon a heaping tablespoonful of the filling into each tartlet shell and refrigerate until chilled, about 2 hours. Garnish with berries just before serving.

Makes 6 tartlets

Ravinia Festival
Highland Park, Illinois

The Levy Restaurants
Chicago, Illinois

Since 1936 the Chicago Symphony Orchestra has spent its summers at Ravinia, a thirty-six-acre wooded park on Chicago's North Shore. Ravinia has an impressive history and presents one of the largest, longest, and most varied summer festival in the United States. World-renowned artists perform orchestral and chamber music, opera, popular symphonic works, jazz, country and folk music, dance, and young people's programs during the ten- to twelve-week season. Concerts are held almost every evening at the Ravinia Pavilion, a spacious structure with a fan-shaped roof supported by a row of slender columns. The Pavilion has unobstructed views for 3,500 patrons inside, and there is additional seating outside on the lawn for 15,000 more. Recitals and chamber music concerts are held in Murray Theatre or Bennett Hall. Most Ravinia patrons enjoy picnics before festival events.

The following picnic was created by Michael Northern of The Levy Restaurants. Many of the thirty-five restaurants created and operated nationwide by The Levy Restaurants can be enjoyed in Chicago, such as Spiaggia, Bistro 110, Randall's Rib House, Eurasia, and Hopper's Dining Car. The Levy Restaurants also provide a variety of food services at the Ravinia Festival, including restaurant dining, buffets, grilled carryout, and picnics to go.

Picnic at Ravinia

Bistro Roasted Garlic

Grilled Fillets of Salmon with Gazpacho Salsa

Bistro Chocolate Cake

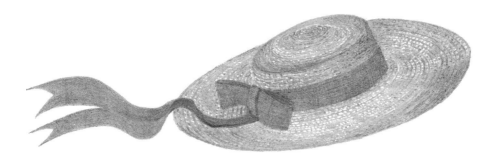

Bistro Roasted Garlic

Baked garlic heads make a delicious spread. Squeeze the garlic out of the skin and spread on slices of baguette.

3 whole heads garlic
1 tablespoon olive oil
Salt and pepper to taste
1 baguette, sliced

Preheat the oven to 350°F. Using a sharp knife, trim the roots from the garlic heads and cut off the tops of the bulbs, exposing the individual garlic cloves.

In a medium bowl, toss the garlic heads with the olive oil and season with salt and pepper. Place the bulbs root-side-down in a shallow baking pan, add ½-inch of water, and cover tightly with aluminum foil. Bake in the preheated oven for 1½ hours until the garlic softens.

Makes 4 servings

The Levy Restaurants

Grilled Fillets of Salmon with Gazpacho Salsa

Six 5-to-6-ounce salmon fillets
2 tablespoons olive oil
Salt and freshly-ground pepper to taste
Gazpacho Salsa (recipe follows)

Light a charcoal fire in an open grill and oil the grill surface well. Lightly coat the salmon fillets with the olive oil and season with salt and pepper. Grill the salmon for 3 to 4 minutes, turning 90° halfway through to make cross-marks. Flip and repeat, cooking another 3 to 4 minutes until the fish flakes easily.

Remove from the grill and place the salmon on a serving dish with the most attractive side up; spoon the gazpacho salsa over.

Makes 6 servings

Gazpacho Salsa

6 tomatoes, cored, seeded, and diced
1 cucumber, peeled, cored, seeded, and diced
½ red bell pepper, cored, seeded, and diced
½ yellow bell pepper, cored, seeded, and diced
½ green bell pepper, cored, seeded and diced
1 red onion, minced
3 or 4 scallions, minced
1 cup extra virgin olive oil
⅓ cup red wine vinegar
Dash Tabasco sauce
Dash Worcestershire sauce
Salt and pepper to taste

The Levy Restaurants

In a colander set over a plate, place the tomato, cucumber, bell peppers, onion, and scallions. Let the vegetables drain in the refrigerator for at least 1 hour, or overnight.

In a large bowl, whisk together the olive oil, vinegar, Tabasco, and Worcestershire sauce. Toss the drained vegetables with the vinaigrette.

The Levy Restaurants

Bistro Chocolate Cake

2 layers devil's food cake (see page 234)
2 cups chocolate frosting (see page 235)
1¼ cups chopped Heath candy bar
2 tablespoons cocoa powder
Fresh berries for garnish

    Prepare the devil's food cake and chocolate frosting. To assemble, make sure the cake layers are level, trimming if necessary. Place one cake layer on a serving plate. Using a spatula, spread the top with the chocolate frosting and sprinkle with about ¾ cup of the chopped Heath bar. Place the second cake layer on top, pressing firmly. Frost the sides and top, coating the cake evenly. Sprinkle the remaining candy on top and press it firmly into the sides. Using a strainer or sifter, sift the cocoa powder over the top of the cake until well-dusted. Garnish with fresh berries.

The Levy Restaurants

Santa Fe Opera

Street Tango
Santa Fe, New Mexico

The Santa Fe Opera has celebrated thirty-seven seasons of music under the stars. Blending the classics, overlooked treasures, and significant premieres, the internationally acclaimed festival attracts opera lovers from around the world during its eight-week season. Santa Fe Opera is the result of the vision of director and conductor John Cosby.

Nestled in the foothills of the Sangre de Cristo Mountains just seven miles north of Santa Fe, the festival's spectacular open-air theater overlooks a vast panorama of mountains, mesas, and sky. Operagoers often arrive early on performance evenings to enjoy the scenery and a picnic.

The following picnic was created by chef Marsha Chobol of Street Tango, Inc. Chobol oversees all food service at the Santa Fe Opera. She incorporates regional foods into her menus and delights in introducing opera performers and patrons to the addictive flavors of southwestern cuisine.

Southwestern Picnic at the Santa Fe Opera

*Cold Sliced Breast of Chicken in a Cumin
and Pine Nut Crust*

*Pasta with Grilled Tricolored Bell Peppers and
Avocado Mayonnaise*

Southwestern Spicy Vegetable Empanaditas

Tres Chocolate Bizcochitos with Red Chili

Cold Sliced Breast of Chicken in a Cumin and Pine Nut Crust

Eight 6-ounce chicken breast halves, skinned and boned
1 cup flour
2 eggs
½ cup milk
2 cups dry bread crumbs
1 cup finely chopped pine nuts
1 tablespoon ground cumin
1 teaspoon oregano
Salt and pepper to taste
Vegetable oil for frying

Wash the chicken pieces and pat dry with paper towels. Place the flour in a small bowl. In another small bowl, whisk together the eggs and milk. In a third bowl, stir together the breadcrumbs, pine nuts, cumin, oregano, salt, and pepper. Dip each chicken breast first into the flour, then the egg mixture, and finally into the bread crumb mixture, coating the chicken well.

In a large, heavy skillet, add the oil to a depth of about 1 inch and heat until hot but not smoking. Carefully place the chicken in the hot oil, leaving plenty of space between the pieces. Fry, turning once, until the chicken is golden brown and fully cooked, about 10 to 15 minutes. Drain on paper towels. When slightly cooled, slice each chicken breast crosswise into 5 slices. Arrange on a serving platter and refrigerate until ready to pack for the picnic.

Makes 8 servings

Pasta with Grilled Tricolored Bell Peppers and Avocado Mayonnaise

¼ cup olive oil
1 large yellow onion, halved and sliced into strips
1 red bell pepper, cored, seeded, and julienned
1 yellow bell pepper, cored, seeded, and julienned
1 green bell pepper, cored, seeded, and julienned
1 pound medium-sized pasta, such as rotelle or shells
Avocado Mayonnaise (recipe follows)

In a large, heavy skillet, heat 2 tablespoons of the olive oil over medium-high heat. Add the onion and bell peppers, and sauté until slightly soft and nicely browned, about 10 minutes. Set aside.

Bring a large pot of salted water to a boil. Cook the pasta until done; drain. Toss the pasta with the remaining 2 tablespoons of the olive oil. Add the cooked vegetables and avocado mayonnaise, and toss lightly. Refrigerate until ready to pack for the picnic.

Makes 8 servings

Avocado Mayonnaise

1 small serrano or jalapeño pepper, chopped
2 garlic cloves, chopped
2 large ripe Haas avocados, pitted, peeled, and sliced
⅓ cup fresh lime juice
⅓ cup white wine vinegar
2 cups vegetable oil
1 teaspoon salt
Freshly ground black pepper to taste

In a food processor with the motor running, drop the hot pepper and garlic through the feed tube to mince. Add the avocados and purée. Add the lime juice, vinegar, salt, and pepper, and process until thoroughly blended. With the motor still running, slowly drizzle the oil through the feed tube until the mixture emulsifies. (This recipe may also be made with a blender.)

Makes about 2½ cups

Southwestern Spicy Vegetable Empanaditas

Unbaked empanaditas can be stored in a sealed plastic bag and frozen until ready to use.

2 tablespoons peanut oil
2 carrots, peeled and diced
½ small head green cabbage, cored and diced
½ red bell pepper, cored, seeded, and diced
1 hot New Mexican green chili, cored, seeded, and diced
2 green onions, diced
2 garlic cloves, minced
½ tablespoon minced fresh ginger root
½ teaspoon ground cumin
Salt and pepper to taste
¼ cup chopped fresh cilantro
1 sheet frozen puff pastry, thawed
1 egg yolk
3 tablespoons water

In a large sauté pan or skillet, heat the peanut oil and sauté the carrots, cabbage, bell pepper, chili, green onions, garlic, ginger, cumin, salt, and pepper until slightly limp, about 10 minutes. Stir in the cilantro and set aside.

On a work surface, spread out the puff pastry sheet. Using a 3½-inch round cookie cutter, cut 9 rounds from the sheet of pastry. Using your fingertip, moisten the edge of each pastry round with water. Place about 1½ tablespoons of filling on the lower half of each pastry round and fold the top over the bottom, matching edges. Press the edges together to seal, and crimp with the tines of a fork.

Place the empanaditas on a baking sheet covered with parchment paper. In a small bowl, beat together the egg yolk and water. Brush the empanaditas with the egg and water mixture, and cut a small vent in the top of each one. Refrigerate the tray for 1 hour.

Preheat the oven to 425°F. Bake the empanaditas until golden brown, about 20 to 30 minutes. Let cool and refrigerate until ready to pack for the picnic.

Makes 18 empanaditas

Tres Chocolate Bizcochitos with Red Chili

Be careful not to overbake these deliciously soft and chewy cookies.

2 ounces unsweetened chocolate, broken into pieces
6 ounces semisweet chocolate, broken into pieces
2 tablespoons butter
2 eggs
¾ cup sugar
3 teaspoons instant espresso powder
1 teaspoon vanilla
¼ cup unbleached all-purpose flour
⅛ teaspoon baking powder
1¼ teaspoons salt
2 teaspoons red chili powder
1 cup semisweet chocolate chips
1½ cups chopped walnuts, pecans, or pine nuts

Preheat the oven to 350°F. Line baking sheets with parchment paper and set aside.

In a double boiler over simmering water, or in a microwave, melt the unsweetened and semisweet chocolate pieces with the butter, stirring to combine. Remove from heat and cool.

In a medium bowl, combine the eggs, sugar, espresso powder, and vanilla, and beat with an electric mixer at high speed for 2 minutes. Add the cooled chocolate mixture, flour, baking powder, salt, and chili powder, and mix at low speed until thoroughly blended. Stir in the chocolate chips and nuts. Working quickly, drop by teaspoonfuls onto the prepared baking sheets. Bake in the preheated oven for 10 to 12 minutes, reversing the position of the tray halfway through the baking time. Let cool on a rack.

Makes 30 cookies

Spoleto Festival U.S.A.

Middleton Place
Charleston, South Carolina

Spoleto Festival U.S.A. is one of the most successful and provocative of American arts festivals. Adventuresome programming includes world premieres, avant-garde events, productions by American artists concerning particularly American themes, and art forms that cross cultural boundaries. More than 125 performances of opera, chamber music, symphonic and choral works, jazz, theater, classical ballet, and modern dance fill historic Charleston during the eighteen-day festival in late May and early June. Concerts are held in Charleston's auditoriums, theaters, churches, courtyards, gardens, and parks.

The Spoleto Festival U.S.A. is a result of the artistic vision of composer Gian Carlo Menotti. Mr. Menotti began the Festival of Two Worlds in the town of Spoleto, Italy, to bring together artists from the North American and European continents. Desiring an American counterpart, he selected Charleston as a festival site in 1977.

The following picnic was created by chef Audrey Aiken of the Middleton Place Restaurant. The restaurant is located on the grounds of Middleton Place, a beautifully preserved eighteenth century plantation and a National Historic Landmark with the oldest landscaped gardens in the United States. The Spoleto Festival Finale begins with picnicking under the live oak trees on the Middleton Place greensward and ends with the closing concert.

Middleton Place Restaurant

Picnic at Spoleto Festival Finale

Seasoned Country-Fried Chicken

Best Deviled Eggs

Pimento Cheese Sandwiches

Marinated Vegetable Salad

Frosted Fudge Brownies

Middleton Place Restaurant

Seasoned Country-Fried Chicken

1 cup unbleached all-purpose flour
2 teaspoons freshly ground pepper
1 teaspoon salt
1 teaspoon paprika
½ teaspoon poultry seasoning
¼ teaspoon garlic powder
1 egg
½ cup milk
One 2½-to-3-pound broiler fryer, cut into pieces and skinned
Vegetable oil for frying

In a plastic bag, combine the flour, pepper, salt, paprika, poultry seasoning, and garlic powder; shake to mix and set aside.

In a small bowl, beat together the egg and milk. Place 2 or 3 pieces of chicken in the plastic bag, and shake well. Dip in the egg mixture; return to the bag and shake again. Repeat with the remaining chicken pieces. In a large, heavy skillet, add oil to a depth of about 1 inch and heat until hot but not smoking. Carefully place the chicken in the hot oil, leaving plenty of space between the pieces. Fry, turning once, until the chicken is golden brown and fully cooked, about 15 minutes. Drain on paper towels and refrigerate until ready to pack for the picnic.

Makes 4 servings

Best Deviled Eggs

The eggs may be hard-cooked and stored unpeeled in the refrigerator for several days before the picnic.

12 eggs
½ cup mayonnaise
2 teaspoons prepared mustard
⅛ teaspoon salt
⅛ teaspoon freshly ground pepper
Paprika for sprinkling

Place the eggs in a medium pan and add enough cold water to cover their tops by 1 inch. Bring the water to a boil over high heat, reduce the heat to low, and simmer for 12 minutes. Place the eggs under cold water, crack the shells and peel, and run the eggs under cool water again.

Slice the eggs in half lengthwise and carefully remove the yolks. In a medium bowl, mash the yolks with the mayonnaise; stir in the mustard, salt, and pepper, and mix well. Spoon the yolk mixture back into the egg whites and sprinkle the paprika on top.

Makes 12 servings

Middleton Place Restaurant

Pimento Cheese Sandwiches

12 ounces sharp cheddar cheese, cut into 1-inch cubes
One 4-ounce jar chopped pimento, drained
3 medium-sized sweet pickles
½ cup mayonnaise
1 teaspoon sugar
½ teaspoon salt
¼ teaspoon freshly ground pepper
Two loaves thinly sliced white bread

In the bowl of a food processor, combine the cheese, pimento, and pickles and process for 5 seconds. Scrape the sides of the bowl with a rubber spatula and process 3 to 5 seconds longer. Add the mayonnaise, sugar, salt, and pepper, and process 5 seconds, or until the mixture is well blended. Set aside.

Remove the crusts from the bread and cut into assorted shapes. Spread the filling on half of the sliced bread and top with the rest of the bread.

Makes 2 dozen sandwiches

Note: To make pimento cheese without a food processor, grate the cheese and chop the pickles. Then mix the ingredients with an electric mixer at medium speed until well blended.

Middleton Place Restaurant

Marinated Vegetable Salad

½ bunch (about 1 pound) fresh broccoli, cut into florets
⅔ pound asparagus, cut into 2-inch diagonal slices
1 small head cauliflower, broken into florets
1 zucchini, julienned
1 cucumber, peeled and sliced
Marinade (recipe follows)
2 heads Boston lettuce
Tomato wedges for garnish

Arrange the broccoli in a steaming rack and place in a pot with 1 inch of water. Cover the pot and bring the water to a boil; steam for 5 minutes, until crisp-tender. Run under cold water and drain. Repeat this procedure with the asparagus and cauliflower.

Place the steamed vegetables, zucchini, and cucumber in a plastic bag and pour in the marinade; fasten the bag tightly. Gently turn the bag until the vegetables are evenly coated. Refrigerate 3 hours or overnight, turning the bag once or twice.

To serve, pour the vegetables into a colander and drain thoroughly. Line a salad bowl with lettuce leaves and top with the vegetables. Garnish with tomato wedges.

Makes 12 servings

Middleton Place Restaurant

Marinade

¾ cup olive oil
3 tablespoons fresh lemon juice
1½ tablespoons white wine vinegar
½ teaspoon Worcestershire sauce
⅛ teaspoon Tabasco sauce
1 garlic clove, minced
½ teaspoon freshly ground black pepper
1 teaspoon grated onion

In a small bowl, whisk together all the ingredients.

Makes 1 cup

Middleton Place Restaurant

Frosted Fudge Brownies

1 cup vegetable shortening
Four 1-ounce squares unsweetened chocolate
2 cups sugar
4 eggs, beaten
1 teaspoon vanilla extract
1½ cups unbleached all-purpose flour
½ teaspoon salt
1 cup chopped pecans
Frosting (recipe follows)

Preheat the oven to 400°F. Butter and lightly flour a 9-by-13-inch baking pan.

In the top of a double boiler, melt the shortening and chocolate over simmering water, stirring constantly. Stir in the sugar, eggs, and vanilla, and mix well. Mix in the flour and salt. Remove from the heat and stir in the pecans. Spread the batter into the prepared pan and bake in the preheated oven for 20 minutes, or until a toothpick inserted in the center comes out clean. Cool the brownies completely and spread with the frosting. Cut into squares, cover, and store in the refrigerator until ready to pack for the picnic.

Makes 3 dozen brownies

Frosting

Two 1-ounce squares unsweetened chocolate
3 tablespoons boiling water
1 tablespoon butter or margarine at room temperature
3½ cups sifted powdered sugar
½ teaspoon vanilla extract
1 egg

In a medium bowl, stir together the chocolate and boiling water until the chocolate melts. Beat in the butter, sugar, vanilla, and egg until blended and of spreading consistency.

Middleton Place Restaurant

Stern Grove Midsummer Music Festival

Vivande Porta Via
San Francisco, California

Attending free Sunday afternoon concerts at the Stern Grove Midsummer Music Festival has been a popular San Francisco tradition since the mid-1930s. The Grove, a natural amphitheater surrounded by giant eucalyptus, redwood, and fir trees, is one of northern California's favorite concert sites. Programs of ballet, opera, jazz, musical theater, instrumental soloists, orchestra and choral performances, and folk music are presented for the enjoyment of all San Francisco Bay Area residents and visitors. Festival crowds averaging fifteen thousand in number gather to picnic and relax in the magnificent outdoor setting.

The following picnic was created by chef Carlo Middione of Vivande Porta Via. This popular European-style food store and restaurant purveys its own prepared foods freshly made on the premises. Deli cases filled with tantalizing carry-out cuisine are next to tables set for lunch and dinner. Middione's food is acclaimed for its integrity, freshness, and elegant simplicity.

Picnic at the Stern Grove Music Festival

Chicken Cooked under Bricks

Savory Bread Salad

Cauliflower Salad

Orange and Lemon Salad

White Meringues

Vivande Porta Via

Chicken Cooked under Bricks
Pollo Al Mattone

This recipe calls for foil-wrapped bricks to weight down the chicken. A heavy pot with some water in it may be used instead of the bricks, but be sure the pot is safely balanced. The dish may be made a day ahead and refrigerated, but do not slice the meat until just before packing it for the picnic.

One 3-pound chicken
⅓ cup extra-virgin olive oil
1 or more of the following herbs: 4 large sprigs fresh oregano or 2 teaspoons
    dry leaves; 2 large sprigs fresh rosemary or 2 tablespoons dry leaves; 8 large
    leaves fresh sage torn into small pieces or 2 teaspoons dry crushed leaves
1 teaspoon red pepper flakes, or to taste
Salt and freshly ground black pepper to taste
2 foil-wrapped bricks

Split the chicken down the back and splay it open so that it is flat. Tuck the wings behind the back. Place the chicken in a shallow dish and coat both sides with the olive oil, herbs, and red pepper flakes. Cover with plastic wrap and marinate in the refrigerator for several hours. The dish can be prepared up to this point 2 days in advance.

Place a large, heavy frying pan over medium heat for about 2 minutes, then add some of the oil from the marinade. Lay the chicken, skin side down, in the hot oil and sprinkle with salt and pepper. Immediately place the 2 foil-wrapped bricks on top of the chicken.

After 5 minutes or so, remove the weights and lift the chicken gently to see if the skin is turning golden brown and not burning. Reduce or raise the heat as needed, and replace the weights. After about 15 minutes, the chicken skin should look deep golden and crusty. Turn the chicken over and sprinkle on more salt and pepper, if desired. Replace the weights and cook another 20 minutes, for a total cooking time of about 40 minutes.

Remove the chicken from the pan and let cool on a cutting board for 6 or 7 minutes before slicing.

Makes 4 to 6 servings

Savory Bread Salad
Panzanella

This tasty salad is a wonderful way to use slightly stale bread. Panzanella may be served alone or on top of the yellow inner leaves of romaine or butter lettuce.

6 large, thick slices of hard, dry Italian bread (not sourdough)
2 large tomatoes, cored and chopped into ¼-inch dice
⅓ cup virgin olive oil
2 tablespoons red or white wine vinegar
8 large fresh basil leaves, coarsely chopped, or to taste
Salt and freshly ground black pepper to taste

Plunge the bread into a bowl of cold water and let it soak until moist throughout. Drain the bread in a colander for about 15 minutes, then squeeze as dry as you can with your hands. Wrapping the bread in a kitchen towel and rolling it tightly will also help rid the bread of excess water. Tear the bread into pieces about the size of a marble and place them in a container for transporting the salad to the picnic. Add the tomatoes, olive oil, vinegar, basil, salt, and pepper, and mix together. Chill in the refrigerator for about 1 hour, or until the juices are absorbed into the bread.

Makes 6 servings

Cauliflower Salad
Insalata di Cavolfiore

This salad is best served cool and is wonderful eaten with crusty bread.

1 large head cauliflower, washed, trimmed, and cut into small pieces
8 anchovy fillets, coarsely chopped
¼ cup minced parsley
3 tablespoons capers
12 Gaeta or other oil-cured black olives, pitted and coarsely chopped
⅓ cup extra-virgin olive oil
Freshly ground black pepper and red pepper flakes to taste

In a large pot over high heat, bring salted water to a boil. Add the cauliflower pieces and boil for about 5 minutes, or until they are just tender. Drain and spread on a plate to cool.

In a medium bowl, combine the cauliflower, anchovy fillets, parsley, capers, olives, olive oil, and pepper. Mix carefully but thoroughly, cover, and chill in the refrigerator until time to pack for the picnic.

Makes 6 servings

Orange and Lemon Salad
Insalata di Arancia e Limone

4 navel oranges or preferably blood oranges when available
2 very ripe lemons
1 small red onion, peeled and sliced thin or finely chopped
6 leaves fresh mint and/or 6 leaves fresh basil, finely chopped
Freshly ground black pepper to taste
2 tablespoons virgin olive oil

    Peel and remove all the pith from the oranges and lemons, reserving any juices that escape. Slice the oranges into ¼-inch crosswise slices and the lemons into ⅛-inch crosswise slices. Arrange the sliced oranges in a shallow dish, then place the sliced lemons on top in a neat pattern. Pour over any reserved citrus juices from the peeling and slicing. Strew the onion over the oranges and lemons, and sprinkle with mint, basil (if used), and pepper. Drizzle the entire surface with olive oil. Let the dish stand for about 2 hours at room temperature before serving.

Makes 4 to 6 servings

White Meringues
Bianchini

3 large egg whites
Pinch of salt
¾ cup granulated sugar
⅓ cup chopped blanched and toasted almonds

Preheat the oven to 250°F. Lightly butter and flour a baking sheet or line it with parchment paper. To be sure the bottoms of the bianchini meringues do not overcook, place the prepared baking sheet on top of another sheet, doubling thickness on the bottom.

In the bowl of an electric mixer, combine the egg whites and pinch of salt. Beat for 2 minutes at low speed, or until the whites foam, then beat at high speed until the whites begin to stiffen. Add 1 tablespoon of the sugar and beat until the egg whites are glossy and stiff peaks form. Stop the mixer and remove the bowl. Gently fold in the almonds and the remaining sugar. Using a tablespoon, drop little mounds of batter about 1 inch apart onto the prepared baking sheet. You can make the cookies bigger or smaller as you like.

Bake the cookies in the middle of the oven for about 1 hour. The meringues should be firm and dry on the outside and remain as white as possible. They may be a little moist on the inside, but they should not be too moist or they will not keep well. If you plan to store them for any length of time, lower the heat in the oven and continue baking them until they are completely dry.

Makes about 12 cookies

Tanglewood

Blantyre
Lenox, Massachusetts

The Tanglewood Festival is the oldest major summer music festival in the United States and one of the most esteemed summertime musical events in the world. Situated in Lenox, a picturesque New England town in the Berkshire Hills of western Massachusetts, Tanglewood is the summer home of the Boston Symphony Orchestra. The orchestra performs on Friday and Saturday evenings and Sunday afternoons during a nine-week summer season.

Tanglewood also presents chamber music concerts, recitals, open rehearsals, the annual Festival of Contemporary Music, and almost daily concerts by the gifted young musicians of the Tanglewood Music Center. The Boston Pops Orchestra appears annually, legendary folk singers are showcased, and the traditional jazz weekend closes the season. Concerts are held in The Shed, an enormous structure with open sides that seats 5,100; the immense lawn provides listening space to thousands more. Tanglewood's four hundred acres of scenic beauty have been the setting for picnics from the start, and each year almost all of the hundrds of thousands of visitors to Tanglewood bring picnics.

The following picnic was created by chef David Lawson of Blantyre, a nearby inn beloved by Tanglewood audiences and performers. Visitors feel like houseguests in a more graceful era in this lovingly restored 1902 Tudor-style manor house. A menu of classical and innovative dishes are offered in the paneled dining room, and chef Lawson also creates very special picnics for guests attending concerts at Tanglewood. Blantyre is a member of Relais & Chateaux.

Blantyre

A Picnic at Tanglewood

Crostini with Three Spreads
Herbed Chèvre, Ratatouille, and White Bean Purée

Chilled Cauliflower Soup with American Black Caviar

Grilled Tuna and Vegetable Brochettes with French Lentils
and Mustard Vinaigrette

Asparagus Bundles with Jambon Cru and Caper Vinaigrette

Roast Chicken in Herb Marinade

White Chocolate Macadamia Nut Cookies

Crostini with Three Spreads
Herbed Chèvre, Ratatouille, and White Bean Purée

Crostini, Italian for "little crusts," are small rounds of toast topped with various spreads. Serve these crostini in a basket surrounded with the spreads packed in large ramekins or wide-mouth canning jars with lock-down lids.

Extra-virgin olive oil for brushing
1 baguette, cut into ¼-inch-thick slices
1 large garlic clove, peeled

Preheat the oven to 400°F. Brush the olive oil on both sides of the bread slices and arrange them on a baking sheet. Bake until the bread is golden on both sides. When the crostini are cool enough to handle, rub each one with the garlic clove.

Herbed Chèvre

8 ounces fresh chèvre at room temperature
2 tablespoons olive oil
1 tablespoon minced fresh rosemary
1 tablespoon minced fresh thyme
3 tablespoons minced Italian parsley
¼ teaspoon salt
1 teaspoon freshly ground pepper
1 sprig fresh rosemary for garnish

In a medium mixing bowl, combine all the ingredients and blend well with a wooden spoon. Adjust the seasonings to taste and pack the mixture into a ramekin or jar. Decorate the top with the sprig of rosemary.

Makes 6 servings

179

Ratatouille

Wonderful served hot, warm, or cold, this classic dish is best made up to three days in advance so that the flavors have time to meld. Remember to bring a serving spoon to the picnic.

1 sprig fresh rosemary
2 sprigs fresh thyme
1 bay leaf
2 tablespoons olive oil
1 medium onion, minced
1 red bell pepper, cut into ½-inch dice
1 small eggplant, cut into ½-inch cubes
3 garlic cloves, minced
½ teaspoon red pepper flakes
¼ cup tomato paste
½ cup white wine
½ teaspoon salt
Freshly ground pepper to taste
3 tablespoons chopped fresh basil
1 sprig fresh thyme for garnish

Preheat the oven to 375°F. Wrap the rosemary, thyme, and bay leaf in a piece of cheesecloth to make a bouquet garni.

In a medium sauté pan, heat 1 tablespoon of the olive oil over medium-high heat and sauté the onion until translucent, about 5 minutes; set aside.

In a large sauté pan, heat the remaining tablespoon of olive oil over medium-high heat and add the bell pepper, eggplant, garlic, and pepper flakes; sauté for about 3 minutes, working in batches if necessary.

Place the onion, the bell pepper and eggplant mixture, and the bouquet garni in a heavy, ovenproof casserole. Add all the remaining ingredients except the basil and the garnish. Stir gently to combine. Cover the casserole and bake in the preheated oven for about 30 minutes, or until the vegetables are just tender. Allow the ratatouille to cool, then stir in the basil. Season with more olive oil, salt, and pepper to taste. Pack the ratatouille into a ramekin or jar. Decorate the top with the sprig of thyme.

Makes 4 to 6 servings

White Bean Purée

1 cup (about 7 ounces) Great Northern beans
1 bay leaf
½ onion, studded with 1 clove
1 small carrot, peeled
¼ teaspoon dried thyme
Salt and freshly ground pepper to taste
Extra-virgin olive oil to taste
1 small bay leaf for garnish

Rinse the beans, cover with water, and soak them in the refrigerator overnight. Drain the beans and place them in a large, heavy saucepan. Add the bay leaf, onion, carrot, dried thyme, and enough cold water to cover by 1 inch. Bring to a boil over high heat. Reduce the heat to low, cover, and simmer until the beans are very tender, about 1½ hours. Add a little more water as necessary during cooking, and skim any foam that rises to the top. Drain the beans, but do not rinse; reserve the cooking liquid. Remove the bay leaf, onion, and carrot.

In a food processor, purée the beans. For a more rustic spread, use a hand-held potato masher and mash the beans until fairly smooth. Season the purée generously with salt, pepper, and olive oil to taste. The purée will become firm upon cooling; use a little of the reserved cooking liquid to keep the purée somewhat liquid. Place the bean purée in a ramekin or jar and decorate the top with the small bay leaf.

Makes 6 servings

Blantyre

Chilled Cauliflower Soup with American Black Caviar

1 small cauliflower
2 tablespoons butter
1 medium onion, thinly sliced
1 bay leaf
Salt and freshly ground white pepper to taste
1½ cups water
1 cup milk
½ cup heavy (whipping) cream or plain yogurt
Pinch of ground nutmeg
2 tablespoons chopped chives
Squeeze of fresh lemon juice
1 ounce American black caviar

Divide the cauliflower into medium-size florets, reserving a few small florets for garnishing. Peel and julienne the cauliflower stalk.

In a medium-size, nonaluminum saucepan, melt the butter over low heat and sauté the onion until translucent, about 5 minutes. Add the cauliflower florets and stalk, bay leaf, salt, and pepper. Cover and sauté about 3 minutes, stirring occasionally. Add the water, cover again, and cook until the cauliflower is very tender, about 20 minutes. Remove from the heat and discard the bay leaf. Transfer to a blender or food processor and purée. Return the purée to the pan, add the milk and cream, and bring to a boil over high heat. Reduce the heat to low and simmer about 3 minutes, stirring occasionally. Pour the soup into a large bowl, cover with plastic wrap, and chill in the refrigerator.

In the meantime, cook the reserved florets in boiling salted water until tender. Run under cold water, drain in a colander, and dry on absorbent towels. Before placing the soup into a chilled thermos for the picnic, stir in the nutmeg, chives, and a squeeze of lemon juice. Adjust the seasonings to taste, and add a little more milk if the soup is too thick. To serve, place a couple of florets and a teaspoon of caviar in the center of each soup bowl, and pour over the well-chilled soup.

Makes 6 servings

Grilled Tuna and Vegetable Brochettes with French Lentils and Mustard Vinaigrette

1 pound fresh tuna, cut into 1-inch cubes
Assorted vegetables, such as zucchini, onions, peppers, fennel, and
  radicchio, cut into 1-inch pieces
1 teaspoon minced fresh rosemary
Salt and freshly ground pepper to taste
Extra-virgin olive oil to taste
Eight 6-inch wooden skewers, soaked overnight in water
French Lentils and Mustard Vinaigrette (recipe follows)
Lemon wedges for garnish

    Light a charcoal fire in an open grill. While it is burning down, place the tuna and vegetables in a shallow bowl; sprinkle with rosemary, salt, and pepper, and drizzle with a little olive oil. Toss to coat evenly. Assemble the brochettes on the wooden skewers, alternating tuna and vegetables. Grill the brochettes over a hot fire, turn after about 1 minute, and grill for 1 minute more. Take care not to overcook the tuna, which should remain slightly pink in the center. Serve the brochettes on top of the French lentils, garnished with lemon wedges.

Makes 4 servings

French Lentils and Mustard Vinaigrette

1½ cups French green lentils
1 medium carrot, peeled and cut into 1/8-inch cubes
½ small onion, minced
1 bay leaf
1 garlic clove, minced
½ teaspoon salt

Mustard Vinaigrette

1½ tablespoons sherry vinegar
6 tablespoons extra-virgin olive oil
1½ teaspoons Dijon mustard
2 tablespoons sour cream
¼ teaspoon salt
Freshly ground black pepper to taste

Rinse the lentils and place them in a medium saucepan over high heat. Add the carrot, onion, bay leaf, garlic, and salt, and cover with water; bring to a boil. Reduce the heat to low and simmer until the lentils are tender but still a little firm, about 20 to 25 minutes.

Meanwhile, make the vinaigrette: In a medium bowl, combine the vinegar, olive oil, mustard, sour cream, salt, and pepper, and whisk until emulsified.

Drain the lentils, but do not rinse; remove the bay leaf. In a small bowl, combine the warm lentils with the mustard vinaigrette. Season with additional salt to taste. Chill in the refrigerator until ready to pack for the picnic.

Makes 6 servings

Asparagus Bundles with Jambon Cru and Caper Vinaigrette

2 pounds California asparagus, preferably thick-stalked
4 thin slices of jambon cru or prosciutto
3 tablespoons extra-virgin olive oil
Juice of 1 small lemon
1 teaspoon Dijon mustard
1 tablespoon small capers, drained and chopped
Salt and freshly ground black pepper to taste
Italian parsley for garnish
Julienne of lemon zest for garnish

Peel the asparagus stalks, then bend each spear; it will snap in half at the point where the tender stalk becomes tough and fibrous. Discard the tough ends.

Bring a good-size pot of salted water to a boil and cook the asparagus for about 6 to 9 minutes, or until the stalks are just tender when pierced with the tip of a paring knife. Immediately run under cold water, drain in a colander, and dry on absorbent towels.

Divide the asparagus into 4 bundles and tie each loosely with a strip of ham. Place these bundles into a serving dish, cover with plastic wrap, and chill in the refrigerator.

In a small bowl, whisk together the olive oil, lemon juice, mustard, capers, salt, and pepper until emulsified. To serve, spoon the room-temperature vinaigrette over the asparagus bundles. Sprinkle with some parsley leaves and lemon zest.

Makes 4 servings

Roast Chicken in Herb Marinade

This recipe was adapted from the Roux brothers' Poulet Bois Boudran, a dish in the great tradition of elegant country-house cooking. The chicken is best made the morning of the picnic because marinating overnight will overpower the chicken. Serve the chicken thickly coated with the herb marinade, accompanied by crusty, country bread.

Salt and freshly ground pepper
One 3-pound chicken*
2 tablespoons olive oil
White wine for deglazing
Herb Marinade (recipe follows)

Preheat the oven to 400°F. Generously salt and pepper the cavity of the chicken. Truss the chicken and rub the outside with olive oil. Place in a large, oven-proof skillet or roasting pan and roast for 35 to 40 minutes, basting with the pan juices every 10 minutes. After 35 minutes, prick the thigh/leg joint with the tip of a paring knife; if the juices run clear it is done. Remove the chicken from the oven and place it breast-side down on a plate. Pour off the fat from the roasting pan, place the pan on a burner over high heat, and deglaze with the white wine. Add this liquid to the herb marinade.

Remove the breasts and leg/thighs from the chicken while still warm. Cut into 8 pieces and place in a shallow serving dish; spoon over the marinade. Cover loosely with plastic wrap and leave to macerate for 2 to 3 hours at cool room temperature, but not in the refrigerator. Transport to the picnic with the other cold foods.

Makes 4 servings

*A free-range or naturally raised chicken will result in a remarkably tasty dish.

187

Herb Marinade

10 fresh basil leaves
⅔ cup vegetable oil
3 tablespoons white wine vinegar
Salt and freshly ground pepper to taste
6 tablespoons Ketchup
2 tablespoons Worcestershire sauce
5 drops Tabasco sauce
Deglazing juice from chicken
3 shallots, minced
1 bunch fresh chives, minced
1 bunch fresh tarragon, minced
1 cup minced Italian parsley leaves

Stack several basil leaves at a time, roll crosswise into fairly tight tubes, and slice into fine strips. In a large bowl, whisk together the oil, vinegar, salt, and pepper. Add the basil leaves, Ketchup, Worcestershire, Tabasco, deglazing juices, chopped shallots, and chopped herbs, and whisk to combine. Add a little more salt if necessary.

White Chocolate Macadamia Nut Cookies

¾ cup unsalted butter
½ cup packed light brown sugar
8 ounces white chocolate
1½ cups unbleached all-purpose flour
¾ teaspoon baking powder
½ teaspoon baking soda
¼ teaspoon salt
3 tablespoons white sugar
1 large egg
1 teaspoon vanilla extract
½ cup coarsely chopped macadamia nuts

In a heavy saucepan, melt the butter and cook to a light golden brown over medium heat. Immediately remove from the heat and stir in the brown sugar. Chill this mixture in the refrigerator for 45 minutes.

Preheat the oven to 325°F. Butter a baking sheet. Grate 3 ounces of the white chocolate and coarsely chop the remaining chocolate. In a medium bowl, sift together the flour, baking powder, baking soda, and salt. In a large bowl, combine the chilled butter and sugar mixture and the white sugar; beat with an electric mixer until fluffy. Beat in the egg and vanilla, then slowly mix in the dry ingredients. Fold in the grated chocolate, half of the chopped chocolate, and the nuts; stir until combined. Shape the dough into 1½-inch balls and dip the tops into the remaining chopped chocolate. Arrange the balls on the prepared baking sheet and bake for 10 to 12 minutes. Cool the cookies before packing them for the picnic in a tin with a tight-fitting lid.

Makes 3 dozen cookies

Tanglewood
Lenox, Massachusetts

The Tobin Corporation
Maynard, Massachusetts

The following picnic was created by Steve Buxton of The Tobin Corporation. Tobin has been providing food service for Tanglewood since 1988 and offers boxed suppers for picnics on the lawn, dinners at the Tent Club, and dining in the two excellent restaurants on the grounds, Highwood Manor and Seranak Supper Club. Seranak was once the home of Serge Koussevitzky, first conductor of the Boston Symphony at Tanglewood.

A Tanglewood Festival Picnic

Smoked Salmon Croustades with
Cucumber and Fresh Dill

Humus with Pesto Bagel Crisps

Peppered Tenderloin of Beef with
Chilled Sweet Red Pepper Coulis

Lobster and Chive Fettuccine with
Black Raspberry Vinaigrette

Black Beans with Peppers and Cilantro

Curried Rice Salad

The Tobin Corporation

Smoked Salmon Croustades with Cucumber and Fresh Dill

¼ pound (1 stick) unsalted butter at room temperature
3½ ounces cream cheese at room temperature
¼ cup sour cream
6 ounces smoked salmon, chopped
2 tablespoons minced fresh dill, plus sprigs for garnish
2 teaspoons fresh lemon juice
¼ teaspoon freshly ground white pepper
Croustades (recipe follows)
1 medium cucumber, peeled, seeded, and sliced ¼" inch thick

In a 2-quart bowl, cream together the butter, cream cheese, and sour cream. Beat in the smoked salmon, fresh dill, lemon juice, and pepper. Cover and refrigerate for 2 hours before using. Right before serving, spread the salmon cream generously over the croustades, top with the cucumber, and garnish with fresh dill.

Makes 4 to 6 servings

Croustades

8 slices firm-textured white bread, crusts removed
4 tablespoons unsalted butter, melted

Preheat the oven to 400°F. Cut the bread slices into neat triangles. Brush the melted butter over both sides of the bread and place on a baking sheet. Bake in the preheated oven until the bread is golden brown and crisp, about 15 minutes. Remove from the oven, cool, and place in a small decorative tin lined with waxed paper for transporting to the picnic.

Humus with Pesto Bagel Crisps

2 cups garbanzo beans, drained
2 tablespoons warm water
¼ cup extra-virgin olive oil
Juice of 1 lemon
2 garlic cloves, minced
1 teaspoon salt
1 teaspoon ground cumin
Freshly ground black pepper to taste
Bagel Chips (recipe follows)

In a blender or food processor, combine the garbanzo beans, warm water, olive oil, and lemon juice, and process until smooth and creamy. Add the garlic, salt, cumin, and pepper and process until the ingredients are well mixed. Scoop into a small container, cover, and refrigerate until ready to use. Serve as a dip for the bagel chips, or spread humus over the chips.

Makes about 2 cups

Bagel Crisps

5 or 6 plain fresh bagels
½ cup prepared pesto sauce
1½ ounces grated Romano cheese

Preheat the oven to 400°F. Slice the bagels about ⅛-inch thick and place on a baking sheet. Brush the slices with pesto sauce and sprinkle generously with cheese. Bake in the preheated oven until the tops of the bagels are crisp and golden brown. Cool and store in a lidded container until ready to use.

The Tobin Corporation

Peppered Tenderloin of Beef with Chilled Sweet Red Pepper Coulis

Four 5-ounce beef tenderloins
2 tablespoons olive oil
Crushed black peppercorns for coating
Chilled Sweet Red Pepper Coulis
Parsley or nasturtium flowers for garnish

Coat the tenderloins with the olive oil and roll in the crushed peppercorns. In a sauté pan, sear the beef over high heat until brown, keeping the center medium rare. Remove from the heat and chill in the refrigerator until ready to serve.

To serve, thinly slice the beef. Place some of the red pepper coulis on each plate. Arrange the tenderloin slices over the sauce and garnish with parsley or a nasturtium flower.

Makes 4 servings

Chilled Sweet Red Pepper Coulis

2 tablespoons olive oil
4 red bell peppers, cored, seeded, and quartered
¼ cup minced shallots
½ cup dry white wine
2 tablespoons dry vermouth
Salt and freshly ground black pepper to taste

In a large skillet or sauté pan, heat the olive oil over medium heat and sauté the peppers and shallots until tender, about 8 minutes. Purée the vegetables in a food processor. In a sauté pan, simmer the wine and vermouth over medium heat until the liquid reduces by half. Add the red pepper purée to the liquid and again reduce by half. Season with salt and pepper. Cover and chill in the refrigerator until ready to pack for the picnic.

Lobster and Chive Fettuccine with Black Raspberry Vinaigrette

⅔ cup minced chives

1 egg

½ teaspoon salt

2 teaspoon olive oil

1¼ cups unbleached all-purpose flour

Meat from a 1½ pound lobster, cut into 1-inch cubes or pieces

½ cup julienned zucchini

1 tablespoon chopped chives

½ pint black raspberries

Black Raspberry Vinaigrette (recipe follows)

Salt and freshly ground pepper to taste

In a food processor, combine the chives, egg, salt, olive oil, flour and 2 teaspoons of water. Process until the mixture resembles wet sand, about 30 seconds. Remove the dough the from processor and knead until it forms a smooth ball, about 1 minute. Cover with plastic wrap and refrigerate for at least 30 minutes.

Roll out the dough and cut the pasta into quarters. Roll each piece through a pasta machine set on the widest notch and continue to roll the dough through the machine on consecutively narrower settings, ending with the second to thinnest setting.

Run the pasta through the fettuccine cutter on the machine. Cut by hand and hang the pasta to dry, about 30 minutes. Bring a large pot of salted water to a boil. Cook the fettuccine until tender but still firm, about 4 minutes. Drain and cool.

In a large bowl, toss the lobster, zucchini, chives, black raspberries, and black raspberry vinaigrette. Season with salt and pepper. Chill in the refrigerator until ready to pack for the picnic.

Makes 2 servings

The Tobin Corporation

Black Raspberry Vinaigrette

½ cup olive oil
½ black raspberry vinegar
½ teaspoon salt
Freshly ground pepper to taste
½ cup champagne vinegar

   Whisk together all the ingredients and chill in the refrigerator.

The Tobin Corporation

Black Beans with Peppers and Cilantro

6 ounces dried black beans, soaked overnight
2 tablespoons olive oil
1 bacon strips, minced
1 small onion, diced
1 clove garlic, minced
2 ounces chorizo sausage, sliced
½ red bell pepper, diced
½ green bell pepper, diced
2 green onions, chopped fine
Salt and freshly ground pepper to taste
Minced fresh basil, oregano, and cilantro to taste
Sour cream (optional)

In a large saucepan, cook the beans in enough stock or water to cover them for about 90 minutes, or until they are tender. Set them aside in their cooking liquid.

In a sauté pan, heat the olive oil over medium heat and add the bacon; cook until the bacon fat is rendered. Add the onion and garlic and sauté until lightly browned. Add the chorizo and bell peppers; sauté until the peppers are tender, about 10 minutes. Drain the black beans, reserving the liquid. Add the beans to the pepper and sausage mixture along with enough cooking liquid to give the consistency of a thick stew. Simmer until all the ingredients are heated through. Add the green onions, salt, pepper, and fresh herbs. Serve the beans with sour cream, if desired.

Makes 4 servings

The Tobin Corporation

Curried Rice Salad

1 cup white rice
1 teaspoon salt
½ yellow bell pepper, finely diced
½ red bell pepper, finely diced
½ green bell pepper, finely diced
1 small ripe papaya, peeled, seeded, and finely diced
1 tablespoon finely diced mango pieces from Major Grey mango chutney
1½ teaspoons Dijon-style mustard
2 teaspoons curry powder
⅛ teaspoon cayenne pepper
1 tablespoon freshly ground black pepper
¼ cup extra-virgin olive oil
¼ pint cherry tomatoes, halved

In a large pot, bring 4 cups of water to a boil. Add the rice and ½ teaspoon of the salt. Stir frequently until the water returns to a boil. Cook until the rice is tender, 12 to 15 minutes. Drain the rice in a colander and rinse under cold water; drain well and let stand for 15 minutes.

Meanwhile, in a large bowl, combine the bell peppers, papaya, and mango.

In a small bowl, whisk together the mustard, curry powder, cayenne, black pepper, and the remaining 1 teaspoon of salt. Gradually whisk in the olive oil in a thin stream until the mixture emulsifies. Combine the rice with the bell peppers and fruit, pour over the dressing, and toss well. Cover and refrigerate overnight. Add the cherry tomato halves before serving.

Makes 4 servings

The Tobin Corporation

Telluride Music Festivals
Telluride Blue Grass Festival
Telluride Chamber Music Festival
Telluride Jazz Celebration

Bread and Roses Catering
Telluride, Colorado

Telluride celebrates the glorious summer season in the Rocky Mountains of Colorado with several music festivals. All styles of bluegrass and country music are featured at the Telluride Bluegrass and Country Music Festival. Concerts are held outdoors in the Telluride town park in late June, and jamming and swapping of tunes are always part of the three-day event. The Telluride Chamber Music Festival presents performances of classical and contemporary works in the historic Sheridan Opera House for two weekends in August. Chicago blues, big bands, Latin music, and traditional jazz concerts are presented by the Telluride Jazz Festival for three days in mid-August. Concerts are held at the Sheridan Opera House, at various local pubs, and outdoors in the Telluride town park.

The following picnic was created by John Gerona of Bread and Roses Catering. Fresh organic vegetables, free-range chicken, and Angus beef are among the foods that John and Janice Gerona use in their creative French and Mediterranean dishes. Bread and Roses has catered for all the music festivals in Telluride.

Picnic at the Telluride Music Festival

Crudités

Spanish Potato Tortilla

Fresh Ahi Tuna Salad in Pita Pockets

Curried Apple-Walnut-Raisin Strudel

Bread and Roses Catering

Crudités

An assortment of fresh vegetables and dipping sauce is a wonderful start to a picnic.

Raw vegetables such as broccoli florets, cherry tomatoes,
    baby zucchini, green onions, baby carrots, blanched asparagus,
    radishes, mushrooms, and celery
½ cup extra-virgin olive oil
3 tablespoons sherry vinegar
Salt and freshly ground pepper to taste

Assemble a mixture of raw and blanched vegetables, cutting the larger vegetables into slices or strips so they can be picked up and eaten easily.

In a small container, whisk together the olive oil, vinegar, salt, and pepper to make a vinaigrette for dipping.

Makes 2 to 4 servings

Bread and Roses Catering

Spanish Potato Tortilla

This classic dish from Spain is a round, flat omelette containing potatoes and onion. It may be served hot, warm, or cold and is an excellent picnic item.

½ cup olive oil
4 baking potatoes, peeled and sliced into ¼-inch rounds
½ onion, chopped
½ teaspoon minced fresh garlic
½ teaspoon salt
¼ teaspoon freshly ground black pepper
6 eggs

In a large skillet, heat the olive oil until very hot but not smoking. Add the potatoes, onion, garlic, salt, and pepper, and mix well. Reduce the heat slightly and cook for about 15 minutes, turning with a spatula 2 or 3 times. When the potatoes are tender and golden, place a plate over the frying pan and drain the olive oil into a small bowl. Set the potatoes aside in a strainer.

In a medium bowl, beat the eggs together and season with salt. Add the potatoes and onion and mix gently to combine.

In the same skillet, heat 2 tablespoons of the drained olive oil over high heat, until very hot. Pour in the egg, potato, and onion mixture and spread the potatoes evenly. Reduce the heat to low and cook the omelette for about 5 minutes, shaking the pan occasionally to make sure the bottom isn't sticking. When the top of the egg mixture is no longer liquid, place a plate over the pan and drain off the olive oil into a small bowl. Turn the omelette out onto a plate. Return the olive oil to the frying pan. Slide the omelette back into the pan to cook on the reverse side for 2 or 3 minutes. Remove the omelette by sliding it out onto a serving plate. Cut into wedges or squares.

Makes one 10-inch tortilla, or 8 servings

Bread and Roses Catering

Fresh Ahi Tuna Salad in Pita Pockets

2 pounds fresh ahi tuna steaks
2 tablespoons cracked coriander
Salt and pepper to taste
2 tablespoons vegetable oil
¼ onion, diced
3 celery stalks, diced
1 carrot, diced
2 tablespoons chopped fresh parsley
½ cup Aioli (recipe follows)
8 pita pockets
Lamb's lettuce (mâche) or other lettuce for garnish

Sprinkle the tuna with cracked coriander, salt, and pepper. In a sauté pan or skillet, heat the vegetable oil over medium-high heat and sauté the tuna steaks until just opaque in the center; remove from the heat and let cool.

In a large bowl, combine the onion, celery, carrot, and parsley. Flake the tuna and add it to the vegetables. Stir in the aioli, mixing until the salad holds together. Spoon the tuna salad into the pita pockets and garnish with lettuce.

Makes 8 servings

Aioli

3 garlic cloves, minced
1 egg yolk
1 teaspoon lemon juice
½ cup extra-virgin olive oil

In the bowl of a food processor, combine the garlic, egg yolk, and lemon juice. With the motor running, slowly add the olive oil in a thin stream, processing until thick and creamy.

Makes about ½ cup

Bread and Roses Catering

Curried Apple-Walnut-Raisin Strudel

6 tart apples such as Granny Smith or Pippins, peeled, cored, and diced
½ cup (1 stick) butter
⅓ cup raisins
½ cup chopped walnuts
2 tablespoons curry powder
2 tablespoons brown sugar
½ teaspoon vanilla
1 teaspoon flour
1 package frozen filo pastry dough, thawed

In a large, heavy saucepan, melt 4 tablespoons of the butter over medium heat. Add the apples, raisins, walnuts, curry powder, brown sugar, vanilla, and flour, and cook until the apples are soft, about 5 minutes.

Preheat the oven to 350°F. Lay out the filo sheets on a flat surface. Cut each sheet into 3 sections. Gently stack the filo sections on top of each other, and place the stack on a damp cloth. Cover with a second damp cloth so the filo won't dry out while you prepare the strudel.

Spread out 1 piece of filo and brush the top with melted butter. Fold in the sides so the strip is one-third its original width.

Spoon one-eighth of the apple mixture in the bottom right-hand corner of the pastry strip. Fold the corner up to make a triangle, so the bottom edge is now even with the lower left-hand side of the strip. Continue folding up in triangles, as though folding a flag, until the top flap is folded over and the pastry is a many-layered triangle. Brush the end of the pastry with butter and make a tight seal. Repeat with the remaining pastry strips.

Place on a baking sheet and bake in the preheated oven for 10 minutes, or until golden brown.

Makes 8 servings

Victoria International Festival

Rebecca's Food Bar & Restaurant
Victoria, British Columbia

The Victoria International Festival presents more than 25 concerts by outstanding soloists and ensembles in the charming British-influenced city of Victoria during a six-week festival in July and August. The festival owes its existence to the creative efforts of its founder and artistic director J.J. Johannesen who also founded the Johannesen International School of the Arts.

Festival concerts are divided into five series and presented in five different locations four to six evenings a week. *Mostly Baroque* features soloists and chamber ensembles performing masterpieces of the Baroque era in Christ Church Cathedral, a Victoria landmark and one of Canada's largest churches. *Recitals Extravaganza* take place in the McPherson Playhouse, and *Concerti Extravaganza* feature soloists accompanied by the Victoria Festival Orchestra in the University Center Auditorium. *Music of the 20th Century* is presented at the University of Victoria, and *The Stars of Today and Tomorrow* presents student concerts at the St. Michaels University School.

The following picnic was created by Rebecca Stewart of Rebecca's Food Bar and Restaurant. Seasonal menus created by a team of innovative chefs incorporate northwestern cuisine with international tastes to make dining at this acclaimed restaurant an exciting and constantly changing experience.

Picnic at the Victoria Music Festival

Salmon and Papaya Rice Paper Rolls with
Wasabi-Ginger Dipping Sauce

Coconut Corn on the Cob

Apple-Basil Duck Salad

Black Bean Steamer

Fresh Lychees

Salmon and Papaya Rice Paper Rolls with Wasabi-Ginger Dipping Sauce

Four 4-ounce salmon fillets
1 lemon, thinly sliced
1 can chipotle chili, minced
1 cup olive oil
Eight 6-inch rice paper rounds
½ papaya, seeded and thinly sliced
¼ cup chopped fresh basil
Wasabi-Ginger Dipping Sauce (recipe follows)

Place the salmon fillets and lemon slices in a large saucepan and add enough water to cover. Simmer over medium heat for about 5 minutes, or until the salmon is just opaque in the center. Using a slotted spoon, carefully remove the fillets to a platter.

In a small bowl, mix together the chipotle chili and olive oil; set aside.

To assemble the salmon rolls, work with 2 sheets of rice paper at a time, keeping the other sheets covered with a damp cloth. Immerse the 2 sheets in a bowl of warm water; remove them immediately and spread them out on top of each other on a flat surface. The rice paper will become pliable in a few seconds. Brush the top of the stacked sheets with the oil mixture and place a fourth of the sliced papaya at the bottom of the sheets. Place 1 salmon fillet on top of the papaya. Sprinkle with a fourth of the basil. Gently roll the 2 sheets of rice paper once over the filling, fold the sides in, and continue folding to make a tight package. Assemble the remaining 3 rolls in the same manner. Wrap the rolls in plastic wrap and refrigerate until serving. Accompany with dipping sauce.

Makes 4 rolls

Wasabi-Ginger Dipping Sauce

2 cups rice wine vinegar
Grated zest and juice of 1 lime
2 tablespoons sugar
¼ cup chopped cilantro
½ cup finely shredded daikon (Japanese white radish)
2 tablespoons chopped pickled ginger

In a medium bowl, whisk together the sauce ingredients. Store in a sealed container.

Coconut Corn on the Cob

4 ears fresh corn, shucked
2 cups coconut milk
2 teaspoon chili flakes
2 tablespoons toasted coconut
1 cup chopped cilantro or basil (optional)

Bring a large pot of water to a boil. Gently lower the corn into the boiling water and cook until just tender, about 5 minutes. Using a slotted spoon, remove the corn from the pot and let cool. Stand the corn on its stem on a cutting board and, with a sharp knife, cut off the kernels from top to bottom, 3 or 4 rows at a time; set aside.

In a medium bowl, whisk together the coconut milk, chili flakes, toasted coconut, and optional cilantro or basil. Add the corn and toss.

Makes 4 servings

Duck Salad

Chicken or lamb may be substituted for the duck in this salad.

2 duck breasts, skinned and boned
⅓ cup hoisin sauce or oyster sauce
Dressing (recipe follows)
4 ounces pasta
2 cups chopped Chinese cabbage
1 carrot, shredded
1 Asian pear or golden delicious apple, peeled, cored, and thinly sliced

Preheat the oven to 350°F. Rub the duck breasts with the hoisin or oyster sauce and place them in a baking pan. Bake in the prepared oven for 30 minutes; let cool and slice thinly. Pour the dressing over the sliced duck.

Cook the pasta in a large pot of salted boiling water; drain. In a large bowl, combine the pasta, cabbage, carrot, pear or apple, and duck, along with the dressing. Toss to combine the salad ingredients.

Makes 4 servings

Dressing

¼ cup honey
2 tablespoons soy sauce
1 cup apple juice
1 tablespoon ground cumin
1 tablespoon ground coriander
Juice of 1 lime
¼ cup black and white sesame seeds, toasted

In a small saucepan, combine all the ingredients and warm over medium heat, stirring to combine.

Rebecca's Food Bar & Restaurant

Black Bean Steamer

1 Dungeness crab, cut into fourths
24 mussels
1 tablespoon cooked black beans
1 tablespoon freshly grated ginger
1 tablespoon finely minced garlic
1 tablespoon hoisin sauce
1 tablespoon chili paste, or ½ tablespoon chili flakes
2¼ cups rice wine vinegar
2 tablespoons soy sauce
2 green onions, chopped, for garnish

Place the crab and mussels in a 4-quart saucepan. In a medium mixing bowl, stir together the black beans, ginger, garlic, hoisin sauce, chili paste or flakes, vinegar, and soy sauce. Pour this mixture over the shellfish, cover, and steam over high heat until the mussels open, about 3 minutes. Remove from the heat, toss, and refrigerate until ready to serve.

Makes 4 servings

Whistler Resort Festivals

Chateau Whistler Resort
Whistler, British Columbia

The Whistler Resort Festival presents concerts in a beautiful year-round resort setting just two hours north of Vancouver. During the summer there are classical, jazz, international, and country and blues festivals as well as weekend performances by concert and marching bands and daily performances by street entertainers. Performances are held at the Whistler Conference Centre and in various other locations, including a raft and atop Whistler Mountain. Festival visitors often picnic at enchanting Lost Lake nearby.

The following picnic was created by executive chef Bernard Casavant, sous chef Rodney Butters, and pastry chef Christian Mitzel of the Chateau Whistler Resort. The Wildflower Cafe features West Coast-style cuisine—food that is fresh, lean, cosmopolitan, and unconventional. Whistler is the first resort chateau built by the Canadian Pacific in one hundred years and has been voted one of the world's premier resorts.

Picnic at the Whistler Resort Festival

Chateau-Style Indian Candy Salmon

Chunky Gazpacho Lager and Tequila-Laced Shrimp

*Parathas with Chili-Spiced Beef and
Roasted Eggplant Yogurt*

Brioche of Cambozola

Compote of Okanagan Fruits

Chateau-Style Indian Candy Salmon

½ cup rock salt
1 cup brown sugar
1 side fresh salmon, bones removed, skin on but scales removed
1 small package smoking chips

In a small bowl, combine the rock salt and brown sugar; set aside.

Place the side of salmon in a long casserole dish, skin side down. Sprinkle the salt and brown sugar mixture liberally over the salmon. Cover with plastic wrap and refrigerate for 24 hours, turning several times.

Preheat the oven to 100°F. Preheat a cast iron skillet, old pie plate, or baking sheet over medium heat on the top of the stove.

Remove the salmon from the salt and sugar mixture, letting the excess moisture drip from the salmon. Place wet towels on an oven rack in the middle of the oven. Place the salmon on top of the wet towels, skin side down. Spread ½ cup of smoking chips evenly in the cast iron skillet or baking sheet. When they start to smoke, remove from heat, and place the pan or baking sheet on the bottom of the oven.

Baste the salmon with the salt and sugar mixture. Bake for 6 to 8 hours, turning on the overhead fan so as not to set off the smoke detector. Baste the salmon frequently during the cooking period. Check the smoking chips and, if necessary, replace them with new chips prepared in the same way as the original ones. After 6 hours, check the firmness of the salmon flesh. It should be firm, like a ripe tomato. If it is too soft, increase the oven temperature to no more than 200°F, basting until done. Remove from the oven, let cool, and refrigerate overnight. The salmon may be sliced before transporting or at the picnic site.

Makes 6 to 8 servings

Chunky Gazpacho Lager and Tequila-Laced Shrimp

¼ cup tequila

2 tablespoons fresh lime juice

¾ pound large shrimp, shelled and deveined

3 tablespoons olive oil

½ red onion, diced

½ red bell pepper, cored, seeded, and diced

½ green bell pepper, cored, seeded, and diced

1 head of garlic, minced

4 cups tomato juice

1 cup Clamato juice

1 cup chicken stock

Salt and pepper to taste

1 small bunch cilantro, chopped

2 Roma, or other small tomatoes, diced

½ cucumber, peeled, seeded, and diced

Celery sticks for garnish

In a small, nonaluminum bowl, combine the tequila, lime juice, and shrimp. Cover with plastic wrap and marinate in the refrigerator for 2 to 3 hours.

In a large skillet, heat the olive oil over medium heat and sauté the onion, red pepper, green pepper, and garlic until soft, about 10 minutes. Add the tomato juice, clamato juice, chicken stock, salt, pepper, and cilantro. Raise the heat to high and bring to a boil. Remove from heat and add the tomatoes and cucumber. Transfer to a bowl, cover, and refrigerate until well chilled, preferably overnight. Pour into a well-insulated thermos and keep chilled until ready to take to the picnic. Serve in bowls or cups with the tequila shrimp, and garnish each serving with a celery stick.

Makes 8 to 10 servings

Parathas with Chili-Spiced Beef and Roasted Eggplant Yogurt

Parathas are a griddle-fried flat bread eaten throughout India. Serve chili-spiced beef or Indian candy salmon on these shallot- and cumin-flavored parathas accompanied with eggplant yogurt.

8 shallots, peeled and diced
2 teaspoons ground cumin
¼ teaspoon allspice
2 cups whole wheat flour, sifted
1 cup white flour, sifted
½ cup clarified butter (page XX)
⅛ teaspoon salt
2 cups warm water
Chili-Spiced Beef (recipe follows)
Baked Eggplant Yogurt (recipe follows)

In a skillet or sauté pan, sauté the shallots, cumin, and allspice over medium heat until golden brown. In a large bowl, combine the shallot mixture, flour, ¼ cup of the clarified butter, and salt. Gradually add the warm water and knead into a dough. Cover the dough with a damp cloth and let stand at room temperature for 1 hour.

Roll out the dough and brush with the remaining clarified butter. Make a book fold with the dough and turn the dough 90 degrees. Fold the dough 3 more times, turning it 90 degrees each time. On a floured work surface, roll out the dough ¼-inch thick and cut into 24 to 30 small circles with a cutter. In a large, heavy, ungreased skillet heated over medium heat, cook the pastry rounds for approximately 45 seconds on each side, or until lightly browned. Cool to room temperature and package in an airtight container for travel.

Makes 25 to 30 small parathas, or 8 to 10 servings

Chateau Whistler Resort

Chili-Spiced Beef

½ pound beef tenderloin, minced
½ medium red chili, minced
½ small green chili, minced
1 tablespoon Dijon mustard
6 sprigs parsley, chopped
½ bunch chives, chopped
3 tablespoons virgin olive oil
Freshly ground pepper to taste

In a small bowl, combine all the ingredients, cover, and chill in the refrigerator until time to pack for the picnic.

Roasted Eggplant Yogurt

1 eggplant
½ cup plain yogurt
1 garlic clove
¼ bunch parsley, chopped

Preheat the oven to 350°F. Prick the eggplant in several places with a fork and place on a baking sheet. Bake the eggplant, uncovered, in the preheated oven for approximately 1 hour, or until very soft. Let cool, then remove the skin of the eggplant. In a food processor, purée the eggplant with the yogurt, garlic, and parsley. Transfer to a tightly covered container for the picnic basket.

Chateau Whistler Resort

Brioche of Cambozola

Fluted brioche molds, about 3 inches at the top and 2 inches at the bottom, are available in cookware stores, or use 3-inch muffin cups. The dough is easy to prepare, but it does take time to rise; it may be prepared the day before the picnic and refrigerated after it has doubled in volume.

2 teaspoons Fleischmann baker's yeast
6 tablespoons milk, warmed
1 whole egg
1 egg yolk
4 teaspoons sugar
½ teaspoon salt
1⅛ cup bread flour
¼ cup butter at room temperature
1½ ounces Cambozola cheese, diced
2 tablespoon minced chives

In a small bowl, stir the yeast into the warm milk and let dissolve for a few minutes.

In a large bowl and using an electric mixer, preferably fitted with a paddle attachment, beat together the egg, egg yolk, sugar, and salt. Add half of the flour and the yeast and beat until smooth. Add the softened butter by tablespoons, beating until completely incorporated after each addition. Beat in the remaining flour and fold in the Cambozola cheese and chives. Turn out onto a lightly floured surface and knead for about 3 minutes until the dough is smooth and not sticky. Sprinkle on more flour if necessary. Place in a bowl at room temperature, cover with plastic wrap, and let rise until double in volume, about 1½ hours.

Butter the brioche tins or muffin cups. Punch down the dough and cut it in half. Cut each half into 6 pieces and gently form each piece into a round. Pinch one end of the dough and pull it out slightly to form a pear shape. To form a

Chateau Whistler Resort

topknot, roll the tapered end to elongate it; then twist the long end 3 or 4 times into a ball and press it firmly into the body of the dough. As the brioches are formed, place them into the prepared tins and set the tins on a baking sheet. Cover loosely and let rise until slightly more than double in bulk; the dough will swell over the tops of the molds.

Preheat the oven to 375°F. Bake the brioches in the preheated oven for 20 minutes, or until the tops are well browned. Remove from the oven and turn out on racks. Allow to cool to room temperature before packaging in an airtight container.

Makes 12 brioches

Compote of Okanagan Fruits

This compote can be prepared in advance and will keep for 3 to 4 weeks in the refrigerator.

Spice Bag

2 cinnamon sticks
6 cloves
Zest of 1 lemon

5 ounces unsalted butter
2 Golden Delicious apples, peeled, quartered, and sliced
3 tablespoons ginger root, peeled and minced
Juice of 1 lemon
½ pound pink rhubarb, peeled and coarsely chopped
⅔ cup sugar
3 Anjou pears, peeled, quartered, and sliced
½ cup dry sherry
3 tablespoons chopped walnuts

Tie together the cinnamon sticks, cloves, and lemon zest in fine gauze cheese cloth.

In a large pot, combine the butter, apples, ginger, lemon juice, rhubarb, sugar, and the spice bag. Gradually bring to a boil over medium-high heat, stirring frequently. Once boiling, reduce the heat to low and simmer until the apples and rhubarb are soft, stirring occasionally. Remove the spice bag and reserve it.

In a food processor, purée the apple and rhubarb mixture, then strain it back into the pot. Replace the spice bag and add the pears, sherry, and walnuts. Bring to a boil and remove from the heat. Let cool to room temperature, cover, and refrigerate overnight. Remove the spice bag and discard. Place the compote in a tightly covered container for the picnic basket.

Wolf Trap Foundation for the Performing Arts
Vienna, Virginia

Someplace Special, Giant Gourmet
McLean, Virginia

Just a short drive from Washington, D.C., Wolf Trap is the first national park dedicated to the performing arts and is under the jurisdiction of the National Park Service. Varied programs include symphonic works, chamber music, opera, instrumental and vocal recitals, dance programs, jazz, folk, ragtime, bluegrass, and country music. Performances by internationally famous vocal and instrumental soloists and performing groups take place at Filene Center, a dramatic open-sided theater with seats for 3,766 under its soaring roof with room on the lawn for 3,000 more. Two eighteenth-century barns on the property also serve as concert halls; the acoustics are exceptional and the atmosphere casual.

The following picnic was created by Someplace Special, Giant Gourmet. A division of Giant Food Inc., this popular all-gourmet store stocks an array of foods from around the world and provides full-service catering for the Washington metropolitan area. Someplace Special has been Wolf Trap's official caterer for six consecutive years.

Picnic at Wolf Trap

The Mixed Ensemble

Wild Honey Rice Salad

Asparagus Vinaigrette

Fruit Kebabs

Someplace Special, Giant Gourmet

The Mixed Ensemble

Four 2-ounce salmon fillets
Four 2-ounce filet mignons
2 cups court bouillon (see page 233)
Four 3-ounce chicken breasts halves
Lemon Herb Marinade (recipe follows)
Red Pepper Sauce (recipe follows)
Fresh basil leaves for garnish (optional)

In a medium pan, bring the court bouillon to a simmer over medium-low heat. Gently lower the salmon fillets into the liquid. Simmer until firm to the touch, about 7 minutes. Carefully lift out each fillet and set aside. Light a charcoal fire in an open grill. Grill the filet mignons for 3 to 4 minutes per side, or until rare. Grill the salmon fillets for 2 to 3 minutes per side. Grill the chicken breasts for 8 to 10 minutes, turning once. Place the grilled chicken in a medium bowl and pour over the lemon herb marinade; marinate in the refrigerator for at least 2 hours. At the picnic, pour some of the red pepper sauce on individual serving plates and arrange the filet mignon, salmon, and chicken on top. Garnish with fresh basil leaves, if desired.

Makes 4 servings

Lemon Herb Marinade

1 cup olive oil
1 teaspoon chopped fresh basil
1 teaspoon chopped fresh oregano
1 teaspoon chopped garlic
2 tablespoons fresh lemon juice

In a small bowl, whisk together all the ingredients.

227

Red Pepper Sauce

⅓ cup olive oil
12 red bell peppers, cored, seeded, and thinly sliced
1 tablespoon chopped garlic
1 teaspoon Tabasco sauce
2 tablespoons Worcestershire sauce
2 tablespoons fresh lemon juice
Salt and freshly ground pepper to taste

In a large sauté pan or skillet, heat the olive oil over medium high heat and sauté the peppers and garlic for 25 minutes. Transfer to a food processor and add the Tabasco, Worcestershire, lemon juice, salt, and pepper; purée. Store in a small covered container.

Wild Honey Rice Salad

1½ cups cooked wild rice, still warm
1½ cups cooked white rice, still warm
2 tablespoons honey
2 tablespoons fresh lemon juice
1 shallot, minced
¼ cup soy sauce
¼ cup olive oil
Salt and freshly ground black pepper to taste
2 tablespoons chopped fresh parsley
2 tablespoons cranberry relish
2 tablespoons chopped macadamia nuts

In a large bowl, toss the warm rice together with the honey, lemon juice, shallot, soy sauce, olive oil, salt, and pepper. Allow to cool to room temperature and add the parsley and cranberry relish; mix well. Top with the macadamia nuts.

Makes 4 to 6 servings

Someplace Special, Giant Gourmet

Asparagus Vinaigrette

16 trimmed asparagus spears
Vinaigrette (recipe follows)
¼ red bell pepper, cored, seeded, and minced, for garnish
¼ yellow bell pepper, cored, seeded, and minced, for garnish

In a steamer basket over boiling water, steam the asparagus for 3 to 4 minutes, or until crisp-tender. Run under cold water and drain. Pour the vinaigrette over the asparagus and sprinkle with the peppers.

Makes 4 servings

Vinaigrette

2 tablespoons red wine vinegar
2 tablespoons raspberry vinegar
¼ cup olive oil
¼ cup soy oil
1 teaspoon Dijon mustard
1 shallot, chopped fine
1 tablespoon chopped fresh basil
Salt and freshly ground pepper to taste

In a small bowl, whisk together all the ingredients until emulsified.

Someplace Special, Giant Gourmet

Fruit Kebabs

If cantaloupe or watermelon is unavailable, use any summer melon that is ripe.

1 honeydew melon
1 cantaloupe
½ watermelon
4 strawberries
Four 6-inch wooden skewers
Dipping Sauce (recipe follows)

Scoop balls from the melons. Skewer all the fruit, alternating colors. Serve with dipping sauce.

Makes 4 servings

Dipping Sauce

2 cups plain yogurt
¼ cup honey
1 teaspoon cinnamon
Fresh mint leaves for garnish

In a small bowl, whisk together all the ingredients and garnish with mint.

Basics

Clarified Butter

½ cup (1 stick) butter

Cut the butter into small pieces for quick melting. In a heavy saucepan, melt the butter over low heat until it crackles and bubbles. Remove the pan from the heat and use a spoon to carefully skim off the foamy butterfat that has risen to the surface. Pour the clear yellow liquid into a container, leaving the milky residue at the bottom; cover. This butter will keep for months in the refrigerator or freezer.

Court Bouillon

2 cups water
4 parsley sprigs
2 celery leaves
1 bay leaf
¼ teaspoon freshly ground black pepper
A few fennel seeds or aniseeds
½ small onion, cut into quarters
½ cup dry white wine or ⅛ cup fresh lemon juice

In a medium saucepan, bring all the ingredients to a boil and simmer for 20 minutes. Remove from the heat and strain through a sieve; set aside.

Crème Fraîche

1 cup heavy (whipping) cream
2 tablespoons buttermilk or yogurt

Combine the cream and buttermilk or yogurt in a glass container and let sit at room temperature (70°F to 80°F) 5 to 8 hours or overnight to thicken. Refrigerate in a covered container.

Makes 1 cup

Note: The advantage of crème fraîche over sour cream is that it can be boiled and reduced without curdling. It will keep in the refrigerator for about 1 week.

Devil's Food Cake

½ cup unsweetened cocoa
1 cup hot, espresso coffee
½ cup vegetable shortening
1⅓ cups sugar
2 eggs
1 teaspoon vanilla extract
1½ cups unbleached all-purpose flour
¾ teaspoon salt
¼ teaspoon baking soda

Preheat the oven to 350°F. Grease and flour two 8-inch round cake pans.

In a small bowl, mix together the cocoa and hot coffee; set aside. In a large bowl and using an electric mixer, beat together the shortening, sugar, eggs, and vanilla and beat at high speed for about 3 minutes, until light and fluffy. In another medium bowl, sift together the flour, salt, baking powder, and baking soda. Add these dry ingredients slowly to the cocoa mixture and beat together.

Pour the batter into the prepared cake pans and bake for about 25 minutes, until a toothpick inserted in the center of a cake comes out clean. Cool for 10 minutes before turning out the cakes onto wire racks.

Chocolate Frosting

6 tablespoons butter at room temperature
¾ cup unsweetened cocoa
2⅔ cups sifted powdered sugar
⅓ cup milk
1 teaspoon vanilla extract

In a medium bowl, cream the butter. Add the cocoa and powdered sugar alternately with the milk and beat until smooth and creamy. Add an additional tablespoon of milk if needed to reach spreading consistency.

Makes 2 cups

Conversion Charts

Weight Measurements

Standard U.S.	Ounces	Metric
1 ounce	1	28 g
¼ lb	4	113 g
½ lb	8	226 g
1 lb	16	454 g
1½ lb	24	680 g
2 lb	37	908 g
2½ lb	40	1134 g
3 lb	48	1367 g

Volume Measurements

Standard U.S.		Ounces	Metric
1 tbs		½	15 ml
2 tbs		1	30 ml
3 tbs		1½	45 ml
¼ cup	4 tbs	2	60 ml
6 tbs		3	85 ml
½ cup	8 tbs	4	115 ml
1 cup		8	240 ml
1 pint	2 cups	16	480 ml
4 cups		32	960 ml

Oven Temperatures

Fahrenheit	Celsius
300°	148.8°
325°	162.8°
350°	177°
375°	190.5°
400°	204.4°
425°	218.3°
450°	232°

Conversion Factors

Ounces to grams: Multiply the ounce figure by 28.3 to get the number of grams.

Pounds to grams: Multiply the pound figure by 453.59 to get the number of grams.

Pounds to kilograms: Multiply the pound figure by 0.45 to get the number of kilograms.

Ounces to milliliters: Multiply the ounce figure by 30 to get the number of milliliters.

Cups to liters: Multiply the cup figure by 0.24 to get the number of liters.

Fahrenheit to Celsius: Subtract 32 from the Fahrenheit figure, multiply by 5, then divide by 9 to get the Celsius figure.

List of Contributors

The Little Nell
675 East Durant Avenue
Aspen, CO 81611
(303) 920-4600

A Touch of Class Catering
7910 NE 139th Avenue
Vancouver, WA 98682
(206) 256-9318

G. B. Ratto & Company
821 Washington Street
Oakland, CA 94607
(510) 832-6503
(800) 325-3483

Food by LaValle
Winston's Pub & Grill
601 Locust Street
Des Moines, IA 50309
(515) 245-5454

The Elora Mill Country Inn
and Restaurant
77 Mill Street West
Elora, Ontario N0B 1S0
Canada
(519) 846-5356

Summerwood Bed and Breakfast
P.O. Box 388
72 East Main Street
Richfield Springs, NY 13439
(315) 858-2024

The Range Restaurant
P.O. Box 354
The Inn at Jackson Hole
Teton Village, WY 83025
(307) 733-5481

Appetizingly Yours Catering
Rural Route 1
Moffat, Ontario L0P 1J0
Canada
(519) 821-6246

Grano Italica
2035 Yonge Street
Toronto, Ontario M4S 2A2
Canada
(416) 440-1986

Engine Co. No. 28
644 South Figueroa Street
Los Angeles, CA 90017
(213) 624-6996

The Embers on the Bay
5555 U. S. 31 North
Acme, MI 49610
(616) 938-1300

Janet Rogers
26 Mishawaka
Rochester, IL 62702
(217) 498-9447

Auberge Ripplecove Inn
P.O. Box 246
Ayer's Cliff, Québec J0B 1C0
Canada
(819) 838-4296

Balducci's
424 Avenue of the Americas
New York, New York 10011
(212) 673-2600

**Kathleen's Fantastic Food &
Catering**
312 Broadway
Newport, RI 02840
(401) 849-9034

Ces & Judy's Catering
10405 Clayton Road
St. Louis, MO 63131
(314) 991-6700

The Levy Restaurants
980 North Michigan Avenue,
Suite 400
Chicago, IL 60611
(312) 664-8200

Street Tango, Inc.
965 Camino Anasazi
Santa Fe, NM 87501
(505) 473-4968

Middleton Place
Ashley River Road
Charleston, SC 29414-7206
(803) 556-6020

Vivande Porta Via
2125 Fillmore St.
San Francisco, CA 94115
(415) 346-4430

Blantyre
P.O. Box 995
Route 20
Lenox, MA 01240
(413) 637-3556

24 Main Street
Maynard, MA 01754
(508) 897-0660

Bread and Roses Catering
P.O. Box 1514
Telluride, CO 81435
(303) 728-5246

Rebecca's Food Bar & Restaurant
1127 Wharf Street
Victoria, British Columbia
V8W 1T7 ,Canada
(604) 380-6999

Chateau Whistler Resort
P.O. Box 100
4599 Chateau Boulevard
Whistler, British Columbia
V0N 1B0 ,Canada
(604) 932-3928

Someplace Special, Giant Gourmet
1445 Chain Bridge Road
McLean, VA 22101
(703) 448-0800

List of Contributors

List of Music Festivals

Aspen Music Festival
P.O. Box AA
Aspen, CO 81612
(303) 925-3254

Chamber Music Northwest
520 S.W. 6th Suite 1112
Portland, Oregon 97204
(503) 294-6400

Concord Jazz Festival
Concord Pavilion
P.O. Box 6166
Concord, CA 94524
(510) 762-2277

Des Moines Metro Opera
106 West Boston Avenue
Indianola, IA 50125
(515) 961-6221

Elora Festival
P.O. Box 990
33 Henderson Street
Elora, Ontario N0B 1S0
Canada
(519) 846-0331

**Festival International
de Lanaudière**
1500 Boulevard Base-de-Roc
Joliette, Québec J6E 3Z1
Canada
(514) 759-7636

Glimmerglass Opera
P.O. Box 191
Cooperstown, NY 13326
(607) 547-2255

**Grand Teton Music
Festival**
P.O. Box 490
Teton Village, WY 83025
(307) 733-3050

Guelph Spring Festival
P.O. Box 1718
Guelph, Ontario N1H 6Z9
Canada
(519) 821-7570

Harbourfront Centre
410 Queen's Key West Suite 100
Toronto, Ontario M5V 2Z3
(416) 973-3000

**Hollywood Bowl Summer
Festival**
Hollywood Bowl Box Office
P.O. Box 1951
Los Angeles, CA 90078
(213) 850-2000

Interlochen Arts Festival
P.O. Box 199
Interlochen, MI 49643
(616) 276-7200

**International Carillon
Festival**
Rees Carillon
Washington Park
Springfield, IL 62704
(217) 544-1751

JVC Jazz Festival
P.O. Box 605
Newport, RI 02840
(401) 847-3700

New York Philharmonic
Free Parks Concerts
New York Philharmonic
Avery Fisher Hall
10 Lincoln Center Plaza
New York, NY 10023
(212) 875-5700

Newport Music Festival
P.O. Box 3300
Newport, RI 02840
(401) 846-1133

Opera Theatre of
Saint Louis
Loretto-Hilton Center
130 Edgar Road
St. Louis, MO 63119
(314) 961-0644

Ravinia Festival
1575 Oakwood Avenue
P.O. Box 896
Highland Park, IL 60035
(312) 728-4642

Santa Fe Opera
P.O. Box 2408
Santa Fe, NM 87504
(505) 982-3855

Spoleto Festival U.S.A.
P.O. Box 157
Charleston, SC 29402
(803) 722-2764

Stern Grove Midsummer
Music Festival
44 Page Street, Suite 604 D
San Francisco, CA 94102
(415) 252-6252

Tanglewood
Boston Symphony Orchestra
Symphony Hall
Boston, MA 02115
(617) 266-1492

Telluride Music Festivals
P.O. Box 653
Telluride, CO 81435
(800) 525-3455

Victoria International
Festival
103-3737 Oak Street
Vancouver, British
Columbia V6H 2M4
Canada
(604) 736-2119

Whistler Resort Festivals
P.O. Box 100
4599 Chateau Boulevard
Whistler, British Columbia
V0N 1B0 ,Canada
(604) 932-2394

Wolf Trap Foundation
for the Performing Arts
1624 Trap Road
Vienna, Virginia 22182
(703) 218-6500

List of Music Festivals

Index

Index

243

244

Index

Acknowledgments

I would like to thank the many people who made this volume possible.

To fellow musicians Frederick Hodges, piano; James Shallenberger, violin; Julie McKenzie, flute—it was great fun. To recording engineer and friend, Bob Shoemaker, and Mike Cogan of Bay Records for production supervision.

My deepest gratitude to all the chefs, restaurants, and caterers who generously contributed menus and recipes to the cookbook. I would especially like to thank Rodney Anderson of Blantyre for his encouragement. To all of the music festival staff members for their informative and prompt assistance.

To my editor, Carol Henderson, for her good advice and attention to detail. To Jim Armstrong for his numerous contributions and computer assistance. To Steve Patterson for more than a year of work, and sincere thanks to all the rest of the crew at *Menus and Music.* To Eric Bernhoft and Frederick Hodges for invaluable research information.

To Michael Osborne and Tom Komagai, for their wonderful design and for supporting this project so enthusiastically. To photographer Don Tuttle and Arno Ruben of Repro-Media, Inc. To Linda Guthrie and the Dunsmuir House and Gardens, and Bruce Nalezny at the Piedmont Piano Company. To Caitlin Coreris, Julia Parish, and Claire Coreris for recipe testing. To my husband John Coreris for his beautiful drawings and his love.

Sharon O'Connor is a musician, author, and cook. She is the founder of the San Francisco String Quartet and creator of the *Menus and Music* series which combines her love of music, food, and travel. Picnics is the eighth volume in her series of cookbooks with musical recordings.